Mary's Place

Reflections and Recipes

by Mary J. Pelzel

All the Best!
Mary J. Pelzel

NORTH WOODS

Published by
North Woods Publishing
Naches, Washington

Published by
North Woods Publishing
62 Deer Cove Lane
Naches, Washington 98937
phone: 509-658-1057
email: MarysPlaceGifts@live.com
ISBN: 978-0-615-34837-7

Printed in the United States of America

10 9 8 7 6 5 4 3 2 1

Note to the Reader

The recipes, hints and tips provided in this book are presented with the understanding that the publisher author deem them to be accurate.

Every effort has been made to make the book as error-free as possible. However, there may be mistakes both typographical and in content. Use of the information in this book is at the discretion of the reader. The author and North Woods Publishing shall have neither liability nor responsibility to any person or entity with respect to any loss or damage caused, or alleged to have been caused, directly or indirectly by information contained in this book. If you do not wish to be bound by the above, you may return this bo to the publisher for a full refund.

Dedication

To my husband and family who have been with me
every step of the way on my journey of personal growth and discovery.
The wonderfulness of Mary's Place has evolved
because of these special people in my life.

My heartfelt wish for everyone is family closeness that creates
shared memories to be handed down for generations.
The kitchen is a great gathering place for family, friends, fun, and food.
Fill it up and create your own recipes and memories that last a lifetime.

Acknowledgments

A special thank you to Jennifer McCord of Jennifer McCord Associates, Roberta Trahan, and Jeanie James of Shorebird Media. When I contacted my copyright attorney, Michelle Bos, as to whom should I turn for assistance with my manuscript, her response was "Call Jennifer."

I did and immediately knew that I was in good hands. Working with her and her associates has been an enhancing and enriching experience. Her guidance and expertise throughout this project have enabled me to achieve a major milepost in my life—the completion of *Mary's Place: Reflections and Recipes*. I could not have done it without them.

WELCOME TO MARY'S NORTH WOODS

I haven't always been the North Woods Woman. The conversion from refined city girl who loved rose gardens, fine foods and champagne into mountain woman, snake jumper and tick flicker was not fast or easy.

I am, as it happens, a gourmet cook. Before I became the North Woods Woman, I would be telling my story while serving caviar or perhaps toast points with pâté. The mountain woman in me now is more likely to ladle out rattlesnake soup with a side of army ant fritters floating in an elderberry coulis. I am happy to say that my love of champagne has remained uncorrupted. And, because food accompanies every major event in my life, I've included some of my favorite recipes to add a little flavor to my stories.

How did I become the North Woods Woman? Since the beginning of our life together in 1984, my husband, David, and I have loved the beautiful mountains of Washington State. Summer campouts and fishing trips were a real treat, and just not frequent enough. David was always watching the real estate ads in the newspaper hoping that just the right place for us would magically appear. He wanted a cabin in the woods more than anything.

After years of watching and waiting for his dream cabin, he had given up. If one avenue of happiness doesn't work out, then you try something else—right? While on our annual trip to the Oregon coast, he decided it might be better to invest in a beach house than a cabin. At that point in time watching the surf roll in and the occasional seal pop its head out of the water was fun and relaxing. As for me, I knew that the ocean was a great once-a-year visit, but never a full time habitat. Salt water mist, rain, wind, fishy smelling seaweed, and squawking swarms of seagulls that just lay in wait for you to bare your head so they can use it for target practice were not on my list as preferred living amenities.

When you feed the seagulls, there is a follow-through process. The birds get fed and then follow through with some lovely, white, warm, gooey dollops with which to decorate the area. Having been a recipient of more than one of these dollops, I am not appreciative of their attributes.

As we toured the area, we found many houses for sale. Our options were endless. My tablet was full of names, phone numbers and addresses. On the four hour drive home we could talk of nothing else. He said "It's relaxing and beautiful." I said "It's wet and there are no trees."

As I was unpacking from the trip and picking up the morning mess, I spotted a folded newspaper on the table. An item had been circled. A cabin in the mountains on Chinook Pass had just been listed for sale by owner. The ad read: *Chinook Pass yr. round home. Knotty pine, very private.* My first instinct was to throw the paper away. My second thought was that after all of the years of looking, I should probably call on just one more. With that in mind, I scheduled an appointment for us to meet with the property owners and take a look the next weekend.

What a surprise to discover that the owners of the cabin were our neighbors just a few houses away. The area had a woodsy name: "Deer Cove Lane." As we drove down a short pine needle carpet road, we discovered not your typical "cabin". There was a covered hot tub, granite kitchen counter tops, a bathroom/laundry room, sleeping loft, wood stove and a functioning outhouse. It was small, but had potential. There was also a garage-sized guest house. As we walked around the area, I could sense David's excitement. It was the end of February and there was still snow on the ground. Through the stark, bare trees we could see the river semi-iced up and hear it running over rocks along the snow lined banks. A squirrel chattered and ran up a tree. David came up behind me and said, "This is it, isn't it." It was not a question.

Our son, Ron, was visiting that weekend with the grandkids, seven-year-old Alexis and three-year-old Mikie. While we had been gone to look at the cabin, Alexis had drawn a picture of a cabin in the woods. She had not known where we had been. The picture was like a "sign" that the cabin should be ours.

The next day, it was decided a second look was needed, and of course Ron should see it, so back to the mountains we went. A third look was not needed. We purchased the cabin on a handshake and a promise that day. The first important step was to place insurance coverage on the cabin. When the insurance agent asked me questions about the deck, I responded with "What deck?" The snow was so deep that neither David nor I had realized that there was a deck on the back side of the cabin. An alarm of some sort should have gone off in my head at that time, but it didn't.

Later that week the sale was finalized over a shared dinner of my famous Spaghetti Bolognese. It was indeed the start of a great adventure and, to say the least, a lifestyle change.

MARY'S FAMOUS SPAGHETTI BOLOGNESE

This dish is delicious and easy to prepare.
You need only a salad to complete the meal.
Serves 20

½ cup olive oil
3 large onions, finely chopped
2 medium carrots, peeled and finely chopped
1 celery stalk, thinly sliced
2 pounds ground beef
2 pounds ground veal
2 pounds ground pork
1 pound button mushrooms, trimmed wiped clean, and thinly sliced
1 28-ounce can of tomatoes
1 28-ounce can of tomato sauce
¼ teaspoon salt
1 teaspoon sugar
2 tablespoons Worcestershire sauce
3 bay leaves
1 garlic clove, minced
2 cups hearty red wine
5 pounds spaghetti
Grated Parmesan cheese

In a very large soup kettle heat the olive oil over moderately high heat. Add the onions and stir quickly to coat, then add the carrots and celery. Reduce the heat to moderate and cook, stirring frequently until the vegetables have softened, about 5 minutes.

Break the meat into the pan. Increase the heat to moderately high and stir until the meat is cooked through with no pink showing, 5 to 7 minutes.

Add the mushrooms, tomatoes, tomato sauce, salt, sugar, Worcestershire sauce, bay leaves, garlic and wine. Bring to a boil, then reduce the heat to very low and cook at a low simmer, uncovered until all but a few tablespoons of liquid remain and the sauce is thick, about 5-6 hours. Stir frequently to avoid scorching.

Just before serving, cook the spaghetti according to package directions. Drain in a colander.

In a large serving bowl, toss the pasta with half of the sauce. Serve with the remaining sauce and plenty of Parmesan on the side.

IT'S TOO LATE TO BACK OUT NOW!

Our friends said we were crazy, but it's too late now. The move is on! Friday, April 24, 1998, we signed the papers, had the keys in hand, and we were euphoric. Stocked with chicken, champagne and paper plates, off we went to set the stage for our first meal in our new home. David, Mr. Romance, had brought the camera so we could have a picture of him carrying me over the threshold to our exciting beginning of woodland living. Very carefully he analyzed where we would stand and placement of the camera on the hood of our '88 Ford Bronco. The timer was set on the camera and I, with a bottle of champagne in one hand and two glasses in the other, was swept off my feet for the momentous event. Click! The camera did its job. Was I ever surprised to be dumped back on my feet. David had put me down. I was dropped at the door like a sack of potatoes. As we walked inside, I wondered what had happened to Mr. Romance. In his eagerness to go inside, he forgot me!

IT'S A TICK!!

A week later was our first opportunity to spend a night at the cabin. It was beautiful spring weather. The forest vegetation was coming to life after a long winter. After unloading the supplies, it was time to go out and explore. Through the trees we went, around the house, down an overgrown path and even walked to the river. Everything was wonderful. After some general clean up of the surrounding area, it was time to break in the hot tub. We changed into swim suits, grabbed some towels and a bottle of wine.

Okay, now the fun begins. Vegetation was not the only thing coming to life in these beautiful mountains. As happy Hubby gives me a big hug he feels a lump on my back. After a visual investigation he reports, "You have a tick."

Did I remain perfectly calm knowing that there was a horrible blood sucking, crawly type insect that had adhered itself to the tender white skin of my back? Answer: of course not. I've heard all of the horror stories about ticks and disease. Panic was an allowable luxury. "OK, I'll be calm. Get the tweezers, get the whiskey – I'll be fine…" This disgusting creature was huge and it was feasting on me. Who knows how long it had been there—maybe all day. I had not felt a thing. Now I know that when a tick bites you, it injects a numbing agent so that you, as the dinner plate, can't feel it sucking the blood out of you with tiny little straws. My tick was already engorged. He had sucked a lot and as far as I was concerned dinner time was over.

The removal of a tick is not an easy task. The idea is to get it to back out of the nest it has made in you of its own accord. You must leave nothing of it behind in the skin. These insects are carriers of Lime Disease and infection. As I leaned over the sink in the bathroom, David made many attempts to remove the tick. His technique was a little lacking, but the effort was sincere. He tried to smother it with first aid cream. We figured that if it couldn't breathe, it would back out for air. He tried to force it to back out with hot pins. Not a good choice. He tried to burn it out with matches (not my favorite).

He tried to drown it with hydrogen peroxide. This put the fire out that the match had caused, but it didn't rouse the nesting tick. Nothing worked. Meanwhile, I could feel the slight nibbling sensation (at least I thought I could) during the tick munchfest. The only thing left to do was to get in the car and make a mad dash down the mountain to the emergency room of the nearest hospital that was FORTY MINUTES away. I could not lean back in the seat of the car. There was no way I wanted to smoosh my bug harboring back into a seat cushion. So I balanced on the edge of the seat leaning forward for the entire ride to town. During the drive to town, I was remembering my friends warning. Just what have I gotten myself into?

We arrived at the hospital and a very pleasant receptionist said, "And how can we help you today." With a slightly crazed look in my eyes, I placed both of my hands, palms flat on her desk and said, "I have a tick in my back, we've tried everything to remove it and now it's your turn."

I was in luck because it was a slow day at the hospital. Paperwork was done and I was in an exam room in minutes. When the doctor came in, chart in hand, he said that I was his first tick of the season, (an honor that I don't care to repeat) and with a sharp needle and a quick flick, it was removed. It was dead and did not wiggle. All of David's efforts had killed the invader. As we left the hospital, I carried the tick flicking needle with me in a death grip. On the trip home I felt well-armed and prepared for my next tick attack.

Mary Joyce of the North Woods – Mountain Woman – was born. Despite everything, we still enjoyed our day. The evening was beautiful and meant to be spent outside. We shared a great bottle of wine and cooked up some Mountain Style BBQ Burgers.

NORTH WOODS BASIL BURGERS

Sprinkle with ticks for extra crunch.
If you bite them before they can bite you, they can't bite back!

Serves 6

2 pounds ground sirloin
¼ cup wine (Zinfandel or Cabernet)
¼ cup, lightly packed, fresh basil, minced
½ cup minced red onion
¼ cup fine Italian bread crumbs
8 sun-dried tomatoes packed in oil drained and finely chopped
1-2 teaspoons garlic salt
8 fresh basil sprigs, moistened with water to throw on the fire
6 large, seeded sandwich rolls, split
6 slices Monterey Jack cheese
2/3 cup mayonnaise
2 tablespoons prepared basil pesto
Red leaf lettuce leaves
6 large tomato slices
Red onion rings, sliced paper thin
Fresh basil leaves (optional)

Gently combine sirloin, wine, basil, minced onion, crumbs, sun-dried tomatoes, and garlic salt to taste. Divide meat mixture into 6 equal portions and gently shape into patties. Work lightly just until it holds together. The lighter the touch, the juicier and more tender the burgers will be. Toss basil sprigs on the coals, then place the patties on the grill. Cook, turning once. During the last few minutes of cooking, place the rolls, cut side down on the outer edges of the grill to toast lightly. You might like to brush the rolls lightly with olive oil before placing them on the grill. During the last minute of cooking, top each patty with a cheese slice. Make pesto sauce for hamburgers by mixing mayonnaise and pesto in a small bowl. Dress the buns with tomatoes, lettuce, onions and fresh basil leaves and the basil pesto sauce as you like. Serve with lots of napkins.

BREAKFAST IN THE MOUNTAINS

Do you hear that? The roaring, rushing sound of the river in springtime is amazing to hear, especially when you are more accustomed to hearing traffic noise and the rattle of the neighbor's attic fan. The gentle breeze brings fragrances of the pine and fir trees, the river water and other fresh smells of the forest that are sensual and wonderful. The sounds of squawking Stellar jays, melodic songs from robins, varied thrush, and finches, and little chirps of conversation are heard from nuthatches, chipmunks and squirrels. Welcome to a mountain morning. All that is needed is a steaming mug of fresh, aromatic, hot coffee.

Sometimes coffee is the hardest part of making breakfast. There is a coffee pot on the kitchen counter that had been left for us. It is a thermal carafe style that I'm not familiar with, but hey, how tough can it be? I pour in the water, carefully measure some freshly ground coffee beans and push the start button.

The pot blows up! There are coffee grounds everywhere. Some are dry and some are wet. They are plastered to the inside and outside of the coffee pot and my kitchen counter and the wall, too. What happened? I don't know, so I clean up the mess and prepare it again.

When I push start, there is another explosion and another big mess. By this time I have about a half hour into making the coffee and still none to drink. David comes into the kitchen looking for coffee and when I inform him the pot keeps blowing up, he says, "Try putting the top on the pot."

I hate it when he's right—that's once.

Finally, with a large carafe of coffee, two over-sized mugs and big fluffy towels draped over our arms we happily head for the hot tub. The water is warm and it is a glorious morning. It is so very relaxing to sip coffee, inhale and enjoy its aroma steaming from the mug and slowly slide into the water. With my eyes half shut just soaking up the moment, I saw something move by the house—a cute, little, gray mouse scurrying across the floor of the deck and down the stairs to the tall grasses of the back yard.

Now, I have nothing against mice as long as they stay outside. Corky, my 27-pound indoor cat was at the window, eyes wide and tail twitching, and thinking of lunch. She had seen the mouse also. I felt very well protected.

The next step on our picture perfect morning was breakfast. One of my favorites is an easy to fix casserole that is terrific just the way it is, or even better served with bacon, sausage, or ham. Be sure to include a basket full of Monkey-Face Strawberry Muffins on the table.

MONKEY-FACE STRAWBERRY MUFFINS

Monkey-Face berries make great muffins! The name Monkey-Face for strawberries has come down through the family generations. They are strawberries that are distorted and have rough patches of seeds on the exterior. My Dad would always throw them away. So just to be ornery and prove my point, I started making Monkey-Face Strawberry Muffins. After a discussion with a Washington State University consultant, I now know that these berries are caused by a lack of boron in the soil. To correct this problem simply stir one tablespoon of Borax into one gallon of water and sprinkle over the strawberry plants. Only do this once every three to four years. Well, so much for their theory. I did as instructed and still have Monkey-Face berries for muffins!

If you use frozen strawberries, they need to be drained and chopped. I prefer to use Monkey-Face berries.

1¾ cups all-purpose flour
½ cup sugar
2¾ teaspoons baking powder
2 teaspoons grated lemon rind
¾ teaspoon salt
1 egg slightly beaten
¾ cup milk
1/3 cup vegetable oil
1 cup fresh Monkey-Face strawberries (or any strawberries), cut into small pieces
1 tablespoon all-purpose flour
1 tablespoon sugar

STREUSEL TOPPING

¼ cup sugar
2½ tablespoons all-purpose flour
½ teaspoon ground cinnamon
1½ tablespoon butter

Combine first 5 ingredients in a large bowl; make a well in center of mixture.

Combine egg, milk, and vegetable oil, stir well. Add to dry ingredients, stirring just until moistened.

Combine strawberries, 1 tablespoon flour, 1 tablespoon sugar, tossing gently to coat. Fold strawberry mixture into batter. Spoon batter into 6 large (3½-inch) greased muffin cups, filling 2/3 full.

For regular muffins, spoon batter into 12 greased regular-sized muffin cups, filling 2/3 full. Sprinkle with streusel mixture. Bake at 400 degrees for 20 minutes or until golden.

As long as it is still breakfast time, close your eyes and envision a squirrel running across the top wood railing of the patio decking, pottery mugs full of steaming fresh and fragrant coffee, bacon sizzling out on the grill, and a large skillet holds frying potatoes and onions. There is a loaf of bread fresh from the oven awaiting strawberry preserves and a friendly chipmunk is waiting for crumbs.

This is what we call breakfast in the mountains and it doesn't get any better than this. No matter how many times we perform this ritual, it is always a special time to relax and spend the weekend morning hours with family and many times friends.

NORTH WOODS HASHBROWN BREAKFAST

If there is an ingredient that you don't care for, simply substitute what you like. This recipe can also be prepared a day ahead. Bring to room temperature prior to baking.

30 ounces of frozen, shredded hash browns (thawed)
1 tablespoon dried parsley
½ cup sour cream
1 can (10 -ounce) cream of chicken Dijon soup (any cream soup you like will work.)
1 (14-ounce) can of chicken broth
½ cup milk
1 cup chopped onion
1 cup chopped celery
1 tablespoon butter tablespoon
1 cup diced or shredded pepper jack cheese
2 eggs, beaten
For topping: paprika, parsley, grated cheese or breadcrumbs

In a large bowl combine first 6 ingredients. Sauté onions and celery in the tablespoon of butter. Add celery mixture to potato mixture, stir in cheese and beaten eggs. Pour into greased 9-inch x 13-inch casserole dish. Sprinkle with desired toppings and bake at 350 for 1½ hours, until browned and bubbly.

THE PERFECT GIFT!

Let's face it, we are all foodies. Every holiday and gathering with family and friends revolves around food preparation and eating. I have found that the more you get everyone involved in the food frenzy, the more fun you have. Whenever any tasty morsels need to be sampled, well, that is Mattie's job of course. A black lab will never turn down your offering—although she is not wild about tomatoes.

Another family tradition was to get the Moms "snockered" on non-alcoholic wine. This group included my mother, Martha; David's mother, Mary; and a family friend, Mom Betty.

These ladies all took a substantial arsenal of medication. When we would pour wine for others, their wine was a sparkling non-alcoholic, usually peach. My favorite is still Champagne. It is pretty, the bubbles tickle my nose and it is usually good for a nice burp or two. But the Moms all loved their peach wine.

By the time they were on their second glass of wine, their little faces were rosy, their words were a little slurred, and they were absolutely giddy about getting "drunk". Mom Betty would say, "Hey Martha, this wine is starting to get to me." My mother would lick her lips and say, "This is really good stuff." David's mother would giggle and say "I'm not having any more," but hold her glass out for the refill. We have lost Mom Betty (2005) and my mother (2009). We have great memories of fun times and they will never be forgotten.

However, what really made my Mom lick her lips was Lemon Meringue Pie. For her, it was the perfect gift.

I remember one birthday that I gave my Mom one of these pies and a fork and she ate the whole thing. Keep in mind that this was after dinner!

MOM'S FAVORITE LEMON MERINGUE PIE

This pie is amazing! If you would like a simpler version, purchase a 4.3-ounce package of Lemon Jell-O® pie filling and follow the directions for pie on the side of the box.

1 baked 9-inch pie shell
1½ cups sugar
1½ cups water
½ teaspoon salt
½ cup cornstarch
1/3 cup water
4 egg yolks, slightly beaten
½ cup lemon juice
3 tablespoons butter
1 teaspoon grated lemon peel
4 egg whites
¼ teaspoon salt
½ cup sugar

Combine sugar, 1½ cups water and salt in saucepan; heat to boiling.

Mix cornstarch and 1/3 cup water to make smooth paste; add to boiling mixture gradually, stirring constantly; cook until thick and clear. Remove from heat.

Combine egg yolks and lemon juice; stir slowly into thickened mixture. Return to heat and cook, stirring constantly until mixture bubbles again. Remove from heat. Stir in butter and lemon peel. Cover and cool until lukewarm.

For meringue, add salt to egg whites; beat until frothy. Gradually add ½ cup sugar, beating until glossy peaks are formed. Stir 2 rounded tablespoons of meringue into lukewarm filling.

Pour filling into cool pie shell. Pile remaining meringue on top and spread lightly over filling, spreading evenly to edge of crust.

Bake in 325 degrees about 15 minutes, or until lightly browned. Cool on wire rack at least one hour before cutting.

THE "HAIRY ASS"!

Big, inky-black spiders have taken up residence here. They are huge. Some are the size of quarters and I know that I can see hair on their derrière. Be careful where you "smoosh" them. The black smudgy stain does not come out easily. I have searched through my comprehensive book of insects and spiders and have not found these spiders listed. So due to their appearance, I have dubbed them "Hairy Asses".

Now, this is very important so pay close attention. Where might you find a hairy ass? Well, let's see—under the laundry basket or even in the laundry. Under the bathroom scale is usually good for two. The ones in the tub and sink are easy to spot—big, black and wiggly on white porcelain—no problem. The toilet is another story. Be sure to lift the lid and check before you sit. Some surprises are really not good!

There have been many run-ins with these huge and highly visible creatures. The most memorable experience was in learning that some of them jump. The previous owners had been doing some construction work and had removed a 4x4 stud that had been buried in the ground about a foot. They had somehow forgotten to fill in the hole left by its removal. I was barefoot at the time and when this "hairy ass" jumped at me, I jumped backwards. My right foot went toe first into that hole—not good. This mountain woman doesn't jump away from spiders anymore. I make a fist and smash their hairy asses.

Recently, while preparing to do a little ironing, (I do as little as possible so my iron had been sitting on the shelf gathering dust), I roused an eight-legged house guest from slumber. As I poured the distilled water into the reservoir of the iron, the spider crawled out and then ran back inside. I snapped the reservoir top shut. "Gotcha" I thought. WRONG! With my ironing completed, I dumped the water from the iron and there he was floating on an air bubble—alive and well—SMOOSH!

Spiders Over Easy—A Breakfast Entrée? There it goes scurrying across my kitchen counter. SMOOSH! With a napkin I wiped the gooey remains of my uninvited breakfast guest off of the side of my hand. One of the legs was still twitching. It would not have been the first time that a bowl of eggs whipped for scrambling has become a swimming pool for crawly black beasties. I love eggs for breakfast, anyway I can get them. However, side orders of spiders are unacceptable.

Would you like a napkin for your toast? Open it very carefully. The folds of paper napkins harbor not only spiders, but large ants when they are in season. Surprises lie in wait within paper towels as you tear them off and spinning the toilet paper roll only makes them dizzy and walk funny.

While we're on this topic, did I mention that this cabin had not been lived in for about 4 years before we moved in? Can you imagine a great place like this just standing empty? It was empty of people only. Many house guests had moved in to fill the void.

The walls and ceilings are made of knotty pine. The light-colored wood has terrific graining and a darker brown circular pattern of knots that create a very attractive room. One particular evening as we sat in the family room just visiting and studying the patterns in the wood, we realized that some of the patterns were moving. Oh yeah, I'm happy now.

Apparently, we have Mr. and Mrs. Hairy Ass and all related family members sharing our home with us. Having all of the lights on was too much for them. It seemed as if every piece of wood had something crawling on it. These big eyed, eight-legged creatures were heading for cracks and crannies. The same knotty pine finish work was done in the bedroom. If one room is crawling, is another? I spent the night with the blankets over my head. When making the bed in the morning, I found them in the sheets. This mountain woman was real close to going back to town.

Meanwhile, happy Hubby is walking around in dreamland. I just love this place, pinch me so I know it's real. So far in this adventure we've discovered ticks, holes in the ground, mice, and spiders. Now, that's not bad, considering this is only week two!

THE NORTH WOODS CARROT CAKE WITH CREAM CHEESE ICING SPRINKLED WITH CRISPY HAIRY ASS LEGS (OPTIONAL)

It saves time if you trap your spiders earlier in the day and pull the legs off from the bodies. Place legs on a paper towel covered baking sheet and place in the freezer to keep fresh until ready for use. Discard the spider bodies. This cake topping is optional and not for the timid. The following cake recipe is outstanding! Serves 12.

½ cup raisins
¼ cup bourbon
2 cups all-purpose flour
1 teaspoon baking soda
¾ teaspoon salt
¾ teaspoon nutmeg
½ teaspoon baking powder
½ teaspoon cinnamon
¼ teaspoon cloves
2 cups granulated sugar
1 cup vegetable oil
2 large eggs
¾ pound of carrots, coarsely chopped
1 cup pecan halves, toasted and coarsely chopped
Ingredients for frosting:
1 package 8-ounces cream cheese softened
4 tablespoons unsalted butter softened
1 cup confectioner's sugar, sifted
1 teaspoon pure vanilla
½ teaspoon fresh lemon juice

To make the cake, heat oven to 350 degrees. Grease a 10-inch spring form pan (or grease a 10-inch round cake pan; line bottom with wax paper; grease paper. Combine raisins and bourbon in small bowl; set aside.

Sift together flour, baking soda, salt, nutmeg, baking powder, cinnamon and cloves in bowl.

Beat granulated sugar and oil in large mixer bowl at medium speed, until well blended. Add eggs, 1 at a time, scraping side and bottom of bowl after each addition. At low speed, beat in dry ingredients, just until combined. Drain raisins and add with the carrots, and pecans to the batter. At medium speed, beat 5 minutes more until batter is well blended. Pour into prepared pan; bake 1 hour and 15 minutes until toothpick inserted in center of cake comes out clean.

Cool cake in pan on wire rack 15 minutes; remove side of pan. Cool completely. For cake pan, run knife around side of pan. Invert cake onto rack; remove pan and wax paper. Transfer to serving plate.

Make frosting: Beat cream cheese and butter in large mixer bowl until smooth. Beat in confectioner's sugar, vanilla, and lemon juice until light and fluffy. Spread over top of cake.

FRIENDLY GHOSTS?

The cabin is haunted. The thought used to frighten me, but after 10 years of living here, I've learned that we have friendly ghosts. The neighbors have told us that our new home has a history. It's known as the "Old Maids Cabin". The story has it that two lesbian lovers owned the place many years ago when it was just a small two-room rustic cabin. Sometimes, I feel that we have a resident ghost or two. There are very definite feelings in the house. Many times the floor of the sleeping loft creaks and the sound of footsteps can be heard from above.

Occasionally, I will hear a thump as if something had been dropped or has fallen off a shelf. This activity only occurs in the upstairs sleeping loft. When I cautiously have gone up to investigate, I have never found anything out of place until one day, after hearing a loud crash, I ran upstairs and found a framed picture of David and myself laying in the middle of the room. How did it get there? These happenings most generally occur when I am home alone.

Once in awhile David has heard a footstep. This presence has never been felt when there has been other family at the house. I think the "Old Maids" are still here keeping an eye on things. They must find us an interesting and entertaining couple. Why else would they stay? For the food, that's why. When you are feeling haunted, try this delicious snack and be prepared to share it with the ghosts.

SWEET-HOT PEANUTS

Makes 12 ¼-cup servings
(6 for you and 6 for the live-in spirits)

2 tablespoons sugar
2 tablespoons olive oil
1-2 teaspoons chipotle chili pepper
1½ teaspoons chili powder
1 teaspoon five-spice powder
3 cups dry roasted peanuts

Preheat oven to 250 degrees. Line a 15 x 10 x 1-inch baking pan with parchment paper or foil; set aside.

In a large bowl, combine sugar, oil, chili pepper, chili powder, and five spice powder. Add peanuts; toss gently to coat.

Spread peanuts in an even layer in the prepared baking pan. Bake for 30 minutes, stirring twice. Cool in pan on wire rack. Enjoy!

JUST WHAT I ALWAYS WANTED

Indoor plumbing? Yes, we have that. Outdoor plumbing? Yes, we have that too. There is a tiny wood cottage painted dark brown that is located back against the mountain. There is a door with a hook and inside there is a resting place for one. It is very entertaining to hear the comments that people make when they become aware of this building. My Uncle Ed's "Wow, is that what I think it is?" was good. My Dad proudly stated, "Not everybody has one of these."

Realistically, who in this day and age wants one? Yes, we are the lucky owners of an outhouse. This facility is not anyone's first choice (except Dad's), but in an emergency, has on occasion been useful. I remember a particular afternoon when my granddaughter, Alexis, was in need of the bathroom. The indoor plumbing was already occupied, and the poor girl just couldn't dance any longer. All of sudden she says, "Okay, I'll go out there, but I'm not going to look down that hole." Little grandson, Mikie, pops up with "That's okay, I'll look."

The outhouse is now only memorabilia from the past. We have had it cleaned and locked up. Did you know that people make a business of cleaning those nasty things? This is how it works. There is a large truck with a huge, long, snake-like hose. There is also a man in armor and a gas mask to operate this equipment. After he successfully sucks all of the dumplings from the depths of the dark hole with the hose, he triumphantly yells, "Hey lady, we're down to the dirt." Spring cleaning has taken on a whole new meaning!

The routine upkeep of an outhouse requires a special technique. First of all, you leave the toilet brush in the house along with the scouring cleanser. The first cleaning tool you will need is a long-handled broom so that you can stand outside and reach all corners within while you are still without. The idea is to sweep away any hairy asses (big black spiders). Having done that, the next step is white paint. Most things that creep and crawl are black.

By using white paint the creepy crawlers are easily visible and that is what I want. The live-in tree frog is acceptable so don't disturb him. He will help to keep the flies down. Armed with bug spray in one hand and a paint brush in the other, I nervously approach my target. With my mission completed, I'm covered with paint from head to toe, and stand back and view my handy work. Painting is not my forté, and this was my first outhouse job. Challenging as it was I was feeling satisfied with the results. While picking up paint equipment, I observed an eight-legged, white vision floating down from the ceiling. It is a freshly painted hairy ass. With his heavy coating of paint, I know he won't make it far. Last but, not least, I place a small covered bucket of lime inside. The lime is used as a deodorizer. The plan is to sprinkle a scoop full down the hole after you tinkle and the bucket is used to hide your extra front door key under.

After all of this exertion, I was starving. Why did cleaning the outhouse make me think of food? Who knows, but it was close to dinner time so into the kitchen I went. This is what I came up with. These grilled pork and cheese sandwiches have great flavor with the addition of garlic, mustard and crisp bacon.

THE OUTHOUSE INSPIRATION
(GRILLED CHEESE AND ROAST PORK SANDWICH SUPREME)

2 tablespoons olive oil
2 cloves garlic, minced
4 ciabatta rolls, split
2 tablespoons yellow mustard
8 slices Swiss Cheese
8 ounces thinly sliced deli roast pork (or leftover pork roast)
8 lengthwise slices sandwich dill pickles
8 slices packaged ready-to-serve cooked bacon, crisped (or fry up your own.)

In a small bowl, combine oil and garlic and set aside.

Trim tops and bottoms of rolls to make flat surfaces. Brush outsides of rolls with oil mixture. Spread insides of rolls with mustard. Place one slice of the cheese on each roll bottom. Top with pickles. Divide pork evenly among roll bottoms, top with bacon and the remaining four cheese slices. Replace roll tops.

Heat a large grill pan or skillet over medium heat. Add sandwiches. Weight down with heavy skillet. Cook for 2-3 minutes or until bread is toasted. Turn sandwiches over, weight down, and cook for 2-3 minutes more or until bread is toasted and cheese is melted.

Cut each sandwich into four portions. Makes 16 servings for city slickers or 8 servings for us mountain folks.

COUGARS AND DEER ARE NOT GOOD NEIGHBORS!

Deer like bread. (Deer like plants too, but somehow these sweet animals loose their charm when they have a mouthful of my petunias.) Anyway, we would go to the day old bread outlet and buy a grocery shopping cart full of loaves of bread, cinnamon rolls, and doughnuts for the deer for $5.00.

During our first month at the cabin, we would put deer feed and bread under a huge fir tree just outside the kitchen window to coax the animals in closer for a better look. The stairs to the sleeping loft were next to this viewing window. Our nightly routine was to feed the animals, pour a glass of wine, and sit on the stairs to wait and watch. When the raccoons came in, we couldn't believe it. There were only two of them. They were quite large and were sitting like little people under the tree. Each was holding a slice of bread and thoroughly enjoying it.

Our neighbors had plum trees and the raccoons would break the branches of the trees off as they helped themselves to Jim's plums. Shortly after, he live-trapped and relocated them. After nine years of absence, we once again have two huge raccoons nightly to share the buffet.

This is also cougar country. Cougars are often called "Mountain Ghosts" because the stealthy creatures are rarely seen in the open like deer and elk. I have not seen a cougar at the cabin. We have had bobcat tracks in the snow around the place. Our neighbor, Tom, was even able to get a picture of the bobcat as it crossed his property. Up the road about two miles from us, horses have been attacked by cougars. Our dog's kennel has a chain link roof to protect them from cougars. One of those big cats could jump in, pick up a dog, and jump back out. A neighbor that feeds the deer as we do, came home one night to find only half of a deer. The cougars had feasted also. I never want to come home to that.

A local story is told of a man stalking a problem cougar. Rifle in hand he was tracking the animal following the footprints left in the snow. Suddenly, there were no prints. The tracks had stopped. The hunter heard a sound from overhead and looked up just in time to fire one round as the cougar sprang for him. Who was stalking who?

This Spring, we had a cougar move into our area. Sam, our neighbor across the road, heard the big cat screaming in the night. That morning there was a dead deer lying by the mailboxes. Another was found close to Sam's house. A representative from the Department of Game came to inspect the incident and confirmed that both of the deer were cougar kills. These massive, wild cats are masters at survival and not picky as to the meat they eat. We are constantly reminded that we live in the wilderness.

This spicy dish is meant to keep the adrenalin going during the cougar crunch.

SPICY SHRIMP

Serves 6

1 large green sweet pepper, chopped
1 large onion, chopped
½ cup butter
1¼ pounds uncooked large shrimp, peeled and deveined
2 cans (8-ounces each) tomato sauce
3 tablespoons green onions, chopped
1 tablespoon minced fresh parsley
1 teaspoon salt
1 teaspoon pepper
1 teaspoon smoked paprika
½ teaspoon garlic powder
½ teaspoon dried oregano
½ teaspoon dried thyme
½ teaspoon ground white pepper
½ teaspoon cayenne pepper
¼-½ teaspoon chipotle pepper
Hot cooked long grain, jasmine rice

In a large skillet, sauté the green pepper and onion in butter until tender. Reduce heat; add shrimp. Cook for 5 minutes. Stir in tomato sauce, green onions, parsley and seasonings. Bring to a boil. Reduce heat; simmer, uncovered, for 20 minutes or until slightly thickened. Serve with prepared rice.

CHILI POTATO BREAD WITH COUGAR CHEESE

I like to pretend that I'm at the gym toning up my upper arm muscles while kneading bread. If you are enjoying a glass of wine at the same time, it makes the imaging so much easier! Knowing that you are burning up all of these calories while exercising with the dough, doubles the enjoyment you get while indulging in the tasty finished product.

15 minutes later you have beautiful bread dough.

I carry a product called Cougar Cheese in my gift shop. Many people have asked me incredulously how cougar cheese is made. I must assure everyone that I do not, in fact, milk a big cat so that many can enjoy cheese from a cougar. This very special cheese is made at the Washington State University Creamery. It is made by college students. There are many varieties available. Our favorite is the original sharp, dry Cougar Gold Cheese.

I have a favorite bread recipe using Cougar Gold Cheese. It has a velvety texture, great flavor and goes well with most any meal. A meatloaf or chicken, or steak sandwich never had it so good. This is an easy recipe so go ahead, get your hands dirty and have some fun.

Definitely Yummy!

¾ cup warm water
3 cups white bread flour
1½ tablespoons dry milk
1½ tablespoons sugar
1½ teaspoons salt
½ cup sour cream
2½ tablespoons potato flakes
1 package of dried yeast or 2 ½ teaspoons of bulk dried yeast
1 tablespoon chili seasoning
¾-1 cup Cougar Gold Cheese (depends on how much cheese you like)— ½– ¾ cup cubed, ¼ cup grated

Mix water, yeast, and sugar. Let this mixture set while you combine dry ingredients in a large bowl: flour, dry milk, salt, potato flakes, chili seasoning and ½-¾ cup cubed Cougar Cheese. Stir sour cream into water mixture. Using your hands blend the wet and dry ingredient together. The dough will be stiff. Place dough onto floured work surface and knead for about 15 minutes, until the dough is smooth and elastic.

Spray a large bowl with a cooking spray of choice, place the dough in the bowl, turning once to coat the dough with the oil. Place plastic wrap over the bowl and put the bowl in a warm, draft free place. Usually, in the oven is a good place. Just don't forget that the dough is in there rising when you get ready to bake.

About an hour later, after you've had time to finish that glass of wine, it is time to put the dough into a bread pan, or for a more rustic look, you can bake it on a cookie sheet. If using the bread pan, grease liberally with shortening and sprinkle with cornmeal. Shape the dough into a loaf and place in the pan. Make an egg white wash with a mixture of one egg white that has been whipped with 1 tablespoon water. Using a paper towel, dip it into the wash and brush it over the loaf. Sprinkle with the remaining Cougar Cheese that has been grated. Spray a sheet of plastic wrap with cooking spray and loosely cover the bread dough. Preheat the oven to 400 degrees.

Allow to rise until double in size. Place it in the preheated oven and bake for about 25 minutes.

Trust me, this is worth the effort!

MOLE HUNTING

Moles, we have moles. Webster says that a mole is a small burrowing mammal with soft fur. I have never seen one, but you can't fool this mountain woman. Those hills of soft dirt are a dead giveaway. The local co-op feed store has little sticks that look like dynamite that are guaranteed to rid you of the pesky animals. One end of the stick is lit and then the stick is placed in the mole hole. The idea is to smoke the little animal out. Nope, that didn't work. Water torture was our next approach.

If we can't smoke it out, we'll flood it out. The hose ran in that mole hole for 45 minutes. Our front yard sank down 6 inches. The next day there were new, soft hills of dirt piled up.

We talked with a neighbor about this problem. His technique was to place a lawn chair a few feet away from the mole hill. Then load a double barrel shotgun, sit in the chair and wait for his shot. On one such afternoon, after waiting by the hole for hours, he saw the ground begin to move and sure enough there was the mole's head. He fired, but hadn't loaded both chambers and missed his shot. You just can't win! I've decided that mole hills are supposed to be considered part of the landscaping in a north woods yard.

After your man has had a most frustrating day of mole hunting, treat him to a hot fudge pudding cake.

HOT FUDGE PUDDING CAKE

These cakes form a rich, thick sauce on the bottom during cooking. Serve with vanilla or coffee ice cream or a scoop of each. It is indeed a magnificent treat.

6 tablespoons Dutch-process cocoa powder
3 tablespoons unsalted butter, cut into 3 pieces
1 ounce bittersweet or semisweet chocolate, coarsely chopped
1/3 cup all-purpose flour
1 teaspoon baking powder
½ cup granulated sugar
3 tablespoons light packed brown sugar
3 tablespoons whole milk
1 tablespoon vanilla
1 large egg yolk (room temperature)
Pinch salt
¾ cup weak coffee

Have oven rack in middle of oven and preheat to 400 degrees. Coat four 6-ounce ramekins with cooking spray, place on rimmed baking sheet.

In a medium bowl combine 3 tablespoons of the cocoa, the butter and chocolate. Microwave, stopping often to stir, until smooth, about 1-3 minutes. Set the mixture aside to cool slightly.

In a small bowl, whisk together the flour and baking powder. In another small bowl, combine 3 tablespoons of the granulated sugar, the remaining 3 tablespoons of the cocoa powder and the brown sugar, breaking up any large clumps with your fingers.

In a large bowl, whisk together the remaining granulated sugar, the milk, vanilla, egg yolk and salt. Whisk in the cooled melted chocolate mixture, followed by the flour mixture, until just combined.

Divide the batter evenly among the ramekins (about ¼ cup per ramekin) and smooth the tops. Sprinkle about 2 tablespoons of the cocoa mixture over the batter in each ramekin. Pour 3 tablespoons of the coffee over the cocoa in each ramekin.

Bake the cakes until puffed and bubbling, about 20 minutes. Let the cakes cool for 15 minutes before serving in the ramekins (the cakes will fall slightly).

ALL GOD'S LITTLE CREATURES

Meet George

It's time to meet George. Behind the cabin, just to the back side of the fire pit, is a storage shed. It has an absolutely beautiful shrub in front of it called a Napoleon's Plume. This shrub is over six feet tall and has massive amounts of cascading clusters of feathery white flowers that resemble the plume on a hat. The shrub has nothing to do with George. I just wanted to share its beauty with you.

It was a warm Saturday afternoon. After we pulled into the yard, I disembarked from the truck and allowed myself the luxury of a good stretch after the 40-minute drive up from town. As I stretched and looked around, I spotted something hanging on the storage shed door. The door is wood on the top half and wire screening on the bottom half. On the lower half of the door is an adorable, little, round-eared, bushy-tailed animal that resembles Mickey Mouse. He had gotten trapped in the shed and was hanging onto the screening with his cute little feeties just waiting for us to come home and let him out.

"Oh my gosh," I said. "Let's name him George." When we told the neighbors about cute, little George, they said, "Pack rat, get rid of it." We have learned that pack rats (affectionately referred to as packies) can get into everything. I had pack rats nesting under the freezer in the storage shed. They ran along the shelving in there and knocked things off. The little darlings tore all of the insulation from under my extra oven that was also in the shed. Everywhere the rats went, they left little trails of black dumplings. We are now in our tenth year here and totally understand about pack rats. They are no longer cute. Unfortunately, they too are a part of mountain life.

All manner of little creatures show up in strange places. A green Pacific tree frog had found a perch on an electrical outlet box and surprised the heck out me when I went to plug in the smoker one fall afternoon. (I was making duck jerky.) I plugged, it croaked and we both jumped. Another frog, a brown one this time, had hopped into the house at some opportune moment when the door was open.

My black and white kitten, Sylvester, was acting stranger than normal on that particular day. He had his head to the floor as he would crouch/crawl for a step or two and then he would raise up in the air for just a moment and then crouch/crawl on the floor again. This pattern continued as he slowly crossed the kitchen.

Upon closer investigation, I discovered the cause for this sort of behavior. He was following a little frog. As the frog would leap and land, so did Sylvester. If the frog stayed in one place for too long, the kitten's paw would gently pat the frog on the back. The frog would croak and hop again. Where's the camera when you need it? Unfortunately, Sylvester's playmate had to go. With gloved hands, (I wasn't going to touch that frog), I picked up my unwanted house guest and set him outside. The cat would have to find other means of entertainment.

Talking Turkey

Turkeys are not attractive birds and they are not very bright (mind wise) either. I was late for a doctor appointment because a flock of wild turkeys was in the middle of the road and refused to let me pass. I should have kept moving and taken a few of them down the road on the hood of my car, but I stopped and began to honk my horn hoping to scare them away. All I achieved was a flock of very irritated turkeys. They attacked my car. They began pecking at the window glass while looking me straight in the eyes. I honked again and they began to claw at the tires. Wild turkeys have razor sharp spikes on the back of their feet. I was afraid that they would flatten my tires. I could not get out of my car and there is no cellular reception at that location. These birds were big, had their wings flared out, and wanted to play demolition derby with my car. I truthfully, didn't know what to do. After several minutes of this abuse, I saw a car coming toward me. The driver was a woman. She also stopped and put her hands in the air in a motion of disbelief.

I honked, and she honked. It was enough distraction to confuse the turkeys. Both of us kept slowly moving forward and honking. The turkeys ran along-side both cars pecking and kicking. Turkeys are not just for stuffing and putting on a platter at Thanksgiving—they make great TURKEY JERKY!

NORTH WOODS DUCK JERKY

Would you like to know how to make duck jerky north woods style? I am asked for this recipe several times a year. It is very good, but it does take time—usually two days is needed to create the perfect duck jerky. I hate the taste and smell of wild duck, so I have made it my job to disguise both being as I'm married to a duck hunter. He brings them home and I want to throw-up. This marinade is terrific and other meats of choice can be used for smoking in this same manner, especially turkey. Enjoy!

The smokehouse flavors from cherry and/or hickory chips permeate the meat and add 'mouth-watering' taste.

BRINE:

¼ cup salt
¼ cup sugar
2 cups water
1 cup cider
1 cup soy sauce
1 ounce bourbon or brandy
½ teaspoon onion powder
½ teaspoon garlic powder
1 teaspoon grated fresh ginger
1 teaspoon orange peel
6 cloves

This brine is great for any wild game. It is also good for beef, pork and salmon. Use 1 to 2 pounds of meat depending on the strength of flavor you desire.

Trim all fat from meat. Slice meat with the grain about ¼-inch to ½-inch thick. It is easier to slice thin when the meat is semi-frozen. Place meat in the cool marinade and leave overnight or for no less than 8 hours.

Remove from brine and allow to air dry without rinsing. Smoke in your smoker for 12 to 16 hours, depending on how dry you like the jerky. Rotate the racks during smoking for even cooking. Use 3 pans of hickory or cherry chips in the early stages of the drying cycle. I like to sprinkle the meat with fresh coarsely ground black pepper on the top side prior to turning. Turn the meat once or twice during the smoking process.

BUGS
OTHER THAN SPIDERS AND TICKS

Whether you live in town, in the country, in the mountains, or at the beach, you deal with bugs. Mountain bugs are really special because they are what I have to live with. The ants come in an amazing assortment—big, medium, small, black, red, black and red, some with wings and some without. The most impressive, of course, are the giant ants with mandibles that could bite your little finger off. Well almost, they look that big to me! They arrive usually in mid May—flying, crawling, and snapping. When you see the first one, look out. There are lots more on the way. At first you will see one or two, then 10 or 20, then 30 or 40, then too many to count. They crawl everywhere and where they aren't crawling, they are flying.

This is a true, real-life nightmare. I call them monster army ants and they bite. It is a total invasion. If you sit outside in a lawn chair, they are all over you. You can shake them off and brush them off but they come back. They just can't be stopped. Just try to go into the house and get away. I don't think so. Somehow they get in.

Look around and ants are on the window sills, crawling on the door frames, across the kitchen counter, in the window blinds, and on the furniture. We counted 35 on the family room carpet one evening. They by far outnumber the spiders on the walls and ceilings. Cover your head when you go to bed. It won't help. The carnivorous monsters will find you. The red welts that you find on your body in the morning are proof that you were found to be a tasty bedtime snack. They are in the blankets and sheets. You awaken in the night with them crawling across your face. Fortunately, this invasion is relatively short lived. With the onslaught of 80 to 90 degree weather, they start to leave.

The normal sized black, red, and black and red ants usually are only outside under rocks and logs. I don't go looking for those but when working in the yard I always holster up a can of Raid. Just call me Quick Draw and I never miss. Actually, it's pretty funny to watch them pick up their ant babies and try to run away as, with a wicked gleam in my eye, I depress the white button on top of the aerosol can and gleefully spray them. They cannot hide from Mountain Woman the assassin!

Last, but not least, there are the tiny sugar ants. Okay, this is a whole different breed. Never spill anything in the house, not a drop of soda pop, not a grain of sugar, not a cupcake crumb—nothing. One crumb or drop will produce a display of a hundred tiny sugar ants. You don't even have to spill anything. Sugar ants will bring their own crumbs just so they can play in your house. They appear magically from nowhere. However, this mountain woman has learned to work her own magic with traps and sprays. Control of sugar ants is possible, but there has to be a constant vigil. They will come back to fight again. This war is won one battle at a time.

There are many people who eat ants in one fashion or another. I am not one of them. The following crostini without the ants is a great party starter.

BASIL CROSTINI

Garnished with ants (optional)

1 thin French bread loaf
Butter softened for spreading
4 ounces mozzarella cheese
1 very ripe tomato, skinned and seeded. You can substitute canned whole tomatoes.
6 anchovy fillets, (or 12 large juicy ants*) soaked to remove excess salt
6 large, fresh basil leaves
Assorted ants lightly sautéed (optional)

***Note:** *If using ants, presoak them in a quality brandy for 24 hours prior to use. They slide down the throat better and don't tickle so much.*

Cut the bread into thin slices and butter or brush with olive oil on both sides. Lay the slices on a buttered cookie sheet. Or cover a cookie sheet with parchment paper. Slice the mozzarella cheese thinly, and lay a piece on each bread slice. Slice the tomato into small strips and halve each anchovy fillet. Lay both of these criss-cross on each bread slice.

Bake in hot oven 400 degrees for 12 to 15 minutes. Keep a careful watch on the crostini and do not let them overcook. The bread should be toasted and the cheese just melted; if the mozzarella is overcooked, it hardens and becomes stringy. When removing the crostini from the oven, snip a scattering of fresh basil over each one. This is also the time to sprinkle on the ants, if using. Serve while very hot accompanied by a red Italian country wine.

THE RASPBERRY MOTH

There is one springtime invasion that is quite lovely to see. Moths about the size of a nickel with wings that appear to be made of a delicate light blue silk flutter in about the same time as the arrival of the monster ants. They are graceful and fairy-like as they flit around in the sun. When I spot them, I always pause to watch and enjoy their ethereal beauty. Who knows what they turn into. My guess is a four-inch ugly caterpillar that will eat my herbs down to the ground or carry away my cat. I should probably be gassing these winged beauties with insecticide, too.

Only once were we lucky enough to view a raspberry moth. They must be very rare. It was a hot summer day. The grandchildren and I had been exploring outside and catching bugs. We were on a mission and prepared with the appropriate equipment: a tiny butterfly net, blue plastic binoculars, a green plastic specimen box, eight inch plastic tweezers and a chain saw. (Just kidding about the chain saw.) We had been having a quite successful day. The specimen box contained grass, a cricket, and a worm type thing with lots of legs. We had even set a few bug traps out. A bug trap is a glass jar that has been buried in the ground with its top flush with ground level and the lid off. After you camouflage the top of the jar opening with grass, the idea is to hide in the bushes and patiently wait for the unsuspecting bug or bugs to fall into the jar.

As our exploration and search continued, we saw it. There on the white door of the guest house was the most amazingly beautiful moth, about the size of a silver dollar. The body was a burgundy mauve velvet and the antennae appeared to be tiny, feathered, silver leaves. With a wild look in his eye, Michael approached with the net. He sees it as a prize for the specimen box. Alexis screamed, “Don’t let Mikie have it! It is a Raspberry Moth!”

After a little discussion we decided that because of its rare beauty we would let it fly away. We've never been able to actually identify the moth. I'm sure it has an impressive Latin name with twenty-five letters in it, but to us it will always remain the Raspberry Moth.

The beautiful moth is still a winged beauty of perfection . . . which leads us to this next beauty of perfection—the Raspberry Soufflé.

RASPBERRY SOUFFLÉ WITH MOTH WINGS

SPECIAL NOTE: If using moth wings for garnish, be sure to trap the moths early in the day for freshness. For a stunning presentation, simply place a dollop of whipped cream in the center of each soufflé and then gently insert a moth wing vertically into the dollop.
Never try to eat the moth wing, however.
They tend to stick to the roof of your mouth much the same as a popcorn kernel husk can do. It can be quite annoying.

Butter to coat baking dishes
1¼ cups sugar—divided (¼ cup -½ cup -½ cup)
24 ounces fresh raspberries or two10-ounce packages frozen berries
¾ cup butter
2/3 cup all-purpose flour
5 egg yolks
2 tablespoons Chambord or cranberry juice
5 egg whites
Assorted moth wings (optional for garnish) *

Preheat oven to 400 degrees. Thoroughly butter eight 8-ounce ramekins or a 2-quart soufflé dish and sprinkle with ¼ cup of the sugar.

Place berries in food processor or blender. Pulse until pureed. Place in a sieve and press gently to extract juice. Add enough water to yield 2 cups. Combine with ½ cup sugar in a medium saucepan. Bring to a boil over medium-high heat. Remove from heat.

Melt butter in a large saucepan over medium heat. Add flour and whisk well.

Gradually pour hot juice mixture into flour mixture and whisk vigorously. Cook one minute. Remove from heat and whisk in yokes slowly so they don't turn into scrambled eggs. Whisk in Chambord.

Beat egg whites in a clean, dry bowl with a mixer until frothy. Gradually add remaining ½ cup sugar, beating until soft peaks form. Stir 1 cup egg white mixture into raspberry mixture. Fold remaining egg white mixture into raspberry mixture.

Spoon into ramekin or soufflé dish. Bake 20-25 minutes (ramekins) or 30-40 minutes (soufflé dish).

ARE WORMS BUGS?

Worms are beneficial for aeration of the soil. We all know that. They even help to maintain our nutritional health by their presence in the wild mushrooms we eat. Where would we be if it weren't for the worms that we dangle from fish hooks to entice that pan size trout? Our sense of music appreciation and nature is enhanced as a happy robin, with his tummy full, sings after pulling an earthworm from the ground. Most of these silent, slow moving, unattractive freaks of nature are interesting and harmless.

Take the inch worm, for example. My first experience with one was in a woodland meadow. While walking with a friend on a lovely fall day through some tall meadow grass near the river, I spotted something climbing up his blue-jean covered leg. What looked like a small worm would stretch out long and flat and then hump up and then flatten out and hump up again.

In this manner it slowly was making its way up my friend's leg. I am, by this time, a brave mountain woman and take a healthy swing at it. As I'm helping him get up off of the ground because I've dislocated his knee, he tells me that what I have heroically killed is an inchworm. His name is Vern and he is still my friend. However, I felt that he was a little ungrateful and did not properly appreciate being saved.

Prehistoric, dinosaur worm relatives are alive and well deep in the earth at our cabin. In a valiant effort to evacuate a mole from its hole, my husband discovered the ugliest worm or grub type life form that I have ever seen. It lives about a foot underground. This entrée is about four inches in length, dirty white in color and fat. Actually, if my little finger had a large biting apparatus on one end, it would be a look alike. The mole got away but just look what we found living in our own back yard! Oh yeah—something to sauté!

There is one last worm that I would like to mention. These are the acrobats. The spruce worms live in our pine trees and swing from the silken strands of a web-like substance they produce. You can see them hanging and swinging from the branches in the summer. Hopefully, you see them prior to walking under them. Finding them in your hair, your sandwiches, or your drinks is not good. These are very bad worms in that they are slowly killing a lot of trees throughout the mountains. There are large patches of brown trees dying everywhere. There is nothing that humans can do to prevent this tree death. What is needed to control the worms is sub-zero winter weather for an extended period of time in order to freeze them out.

Since the beginning of time, bugs have been a source of nutritional protein and for many cultures, a diet mainstay. Be brave and try the following recipe. I can't vouch for the flavor of the grubs (bugs are not my forté). However, the sea scallops are tender and to-die-for wonderful.

THE JUICIER THE BETTER PAN SEARED GARDEN GRUBS
— OR —
SAUTÉED SEA SCALLOPS IN WHITE WINE & HERBS

½ cup all-purpose flour
½ teaspoon salt
½ teaspoon black pepper
6 boneless, skinless, chicken breast halves
½ pound bay or sea scallops (or large, juicy grubs)
¼ cup olive oil
1½ cups sliced fresh mushrooms
1 medium onion chopped
¼ cup white wine or chicken broth
2 teaspoons cornstarch
½ cup whipping cream
1 teaspoon dried tarragon
½ cup shredded Swiss cheese

In a large resealable plastic bag combine the flour, salt, and pepper. Add chicken and scallops in batches; shake to coat. In a large skillet, sauté chicken and then scallops in oil until lightly browned. Scallops will take less time to cook than the chicken. Transfer to a greased 13-in. x 9-in. x 2-in. baking dish.

In the pan drippings, sauté mushrooms and onion. Add wine or broth. Bring to a boil; cook until liquid is reduced to 2 tablespoons. Combine cornstarch, cream and tarragon until blended. Spoon over chicken and scallops. Sprinkle with cheese. Bake, uncovered at 375 degrees for 18-20 minutes or until chicken juices run clear. Yield 6 servings.

WHY MOUNTAIN WOMEN WEAR HARD HATS

OSHA and related agencies are there to advise and protect one from on the job injury. Who is there to advise and protect against injury in the woods? The answer is no one. You are on your own. It is a trial and error, day by day, learn-as-you-go situation.

Example number 1: Every North Woods Woman goes huckleberry picking. These tiny blueberries have a delicate taste that cannot be described. One has to sample this mountain-grown treasure for oneself. In pancakes, pies, muffins, jam, syrup or right out of the picking bucket, they are decadent. Some years the going price for huckleberries is $50.00 a gallon. That tells you how good they are.

When you go huckleberry picking, there are a couple of things you should know. First of all, be aware that you could be sharing the berry patch with a bear. They like berries too. The second tip is be careful not to trip. After hours of picking to fill a bucket with berries, falling and spilling your harvested treasures down the mountain side as your bucket goes rolling away could bring a grown man to tears. The third tip is that your bucket will fill up a lot faster if you quit eating the berries. The fourth tip is to never wear a blue, furry angora sweater when picking near a hornet's nest. As the hornets chased me out of the berry patch, they became tangled in the furry threads of my sweater. The faster I ran, the louder they buzzed. When help reached me, my sweater was alive with the angry trapped bees. I do believe that hornets are the meanest of all bees and I will never again wear a blue sweater. But, huckleberries are worth the effort.

NORTH WOODS HUCKLEBERRY PIE

Note: The crust recipe (below) creates a wonderful flaky and tasty crust. HOWEVER, a box of premade pie crust sheets from the dairy section at the super market is very good and soooooo easy. Feel free to use that method.

- 4 cups huckleberries
- 1 cup sugar
- 1 tablespoon lemon juice
- ¼ cup tapioca

Mix berries, tapioca, sugar and lemon juice in a large bowl and let stand 15 minutes.

Meanwhile, make the crust.

Ingredients for flaky pastry for 2-crust pie:

- 3 cups sifted all-purpose flour
- 1½ teaspoon salt
- 1 cup plus 2 tablespoons shortening
- 6 tablespoons ice water

Combine flour and salt in mixing bowl. Cut in shortening with pastry blender until mixture is the consistency of coarse cornmeal or tiny peas.

Sprinkle on cold water, 1 tablespoon at a time, tossing mixture lightly (I like to use my hands to do this). Add water each time to the driest part of the mixture. The dough should be just moist enough to hold together when pressed gently with a fork. It should not be sticky. Shape dough into two flat balls with your hands.

To roll the bottom crust: Press one dough ball on lightly floured surface. Roll it lightly with short strokes from center in all directions to ⅛" thick making a 10-inch to 11-inch circle. Fold rolled dough in half and ease it loosely into the pie pan with fold in the center. Unfold and fit into pan using care not to stretch the dough.

Put berries in pastry-lined pan and dot with butter.

To roll the top crust: Roll second ball of dough like the first one (for bottom crust). Fold pastry circle in half; lift it to the top of the pie with fold in center. Gently unfold over top of pie. Trim with scissors to ½-inch beyond edge of pie. Fold top edge under bottom crust and press gently with fingers to seal and to make an upright edge. Crimp edge.

Cut vents in the top crust or prick with a fork to allow steam to escape. You may want to develop your own signature style for marking your crusts. Brush the crust with milk or cream. Dipping a paper towel into the cream works well and then rub it over the crust. Lastly, sprinkle raw sugar or sugar crystals over the crust.

Bake at 425 degrees for 30 minutes or until nicely browned. For a brown undercrust, bake on lowest oven shelf. If the edges of the top crust are getting over brown, cover them with small strips of tin foil to keep from burning.

WATCH OUT! THAT MIGHT HURT!

When people hear that I live in the mountains, one of the most common responses is "Wow, are you ever lucky to live in God's country." Surrounded by the wonders of nature as I am on a daily basis, I do feel lucky. But you know, sometimes nature bites. The emotional upsets, hot flashes and an I'm-going-to-bite-your-head-off attitude during menopause don't hold a candle to the venting and ravings of this developing mountain woman. In actual fact, I should be listed as Hazard Number One.

The obvious, of course, is the mosquito. Our mosquitoes come in two sizes, big and giant. The big ones come in noisy swarms. They attack and bite relentlessly as you swat and bleed. The giant ones usually come at you one at a time and bring a hypodermic needle with which to puncture you. Many a mountain summer evening is spoiled by their need to feed. So, what is the answer? If you sit close to a very smoky campfire, there is some relief. Repellent sprays are like putting syrup on a pancake. The most effective effort for us to date is to actively use a spray apparatus and go into the surrounding underbrush and around the house to spray early in the season. The previous owner of the cabin had told us that this is what you have to do.

On one such occasion, David was doing exactly this. He had, however, neglected to inform me of this activity. Almost every window in the house was open. The house quickly filled up with the insecticide fumes. Coughing and hacking, I shut the windows in hopes of keeping out additional fumes and ran outside. Outside, I can't breathe either.

"What ARE you doing?" I yelled at him. Mountain Man proudly raises his spray wand and says "I'm killing mosquitoes". "Well, you're killing me too," I said as I trounced off down the lane and perched myself on a rock to view the remainder of the proceedings. Many hours later, we were still trying to rid the house of the fumes caused by this bug annihilation rampage. He never did that again. Once was enough.

When planning for your outdoor barbecue, there is one condiment for your hamburgers and hotdogs that you will not have to supply. The wasps and hornets won't wait for an invitation and they don't stand on ceremony as they show up and help themselves to several servings. The uninformed say, "That's okay. They don't eat much."

YES, THEY DO! These meat eaters will break off big chunks of my lunch and fly off with it. If you slap at them, then they break off big chunks of you! Many is the time that they have actually chased our outdoor party inside. For this reason, we have trees that are decorated in the summer months with yellow plastic hanging wasp traps that are filled with fluid that hopefully smells better than your barbecue to the wasps. We have found that apple juice is a favorite. If you want some for yourself, drink it in the house.

If you think you like crab cakes (I love crab cakes!), just try to enjoy and not share this amazing treat with your winged friends.

CURRIED CRAB CAKES

2 eggs, lightly beaten
½ cup sour cream
1 tablespoon curry powder
1 tablespoon Worcestershire sauce
1 teaspoon stone ground mustard
¾ cup Parmesan bread crumbs
¼ cup finely chopped red sweet pepper
¼ cup finely chopped green sweet pepper
¼ cup finely chopped red onion
¼ cup thinly sliced green onions
2 tablespoons snipped fresh parsley
1 pound cooked lump crabmeat, flaked or three 6-ounce cans crabmeat drained, flaked, and cartilage removed (about 3 cups)
2 tablespoons olive oil

In a large bowl combine eggs, sour cream, curry powder, Worcestershire sauce, and mustard. Stir in bread crumbs, red and green sweet peppers, red onion, green onions, and parsley. Add crabmeat; mix well. Shape crab mixture into twelve ½-inch-thick patties.

In a very large skillet, heat oil over medium heat. Add half of the crab cakes; cook about 6 minutes or until golden brown and heated through, turning once. If cakes brown too quickly, reduce heat. Keep warm in a 300 degrees oven while cooking remaining crab cakes. Add additional oil if necessary.

Your crab cakes are already tasty. However serving them with Mango Salsa will only increase the pleasure of eating the crab cakes.

MANGO SALSA

Take my advice and serve this marvelous meal inside. I have learned the hard way that even the bugs love curried crab cakes with mango salsa!

In a medium bowl, combine:

1½ cups chopped, peeled mangoes
1 medium red sweet pepper, finely chopped
¼ cup thinly sliced green onions
1 fresh jalapeno chili pepper, seeded and finely chopped
½ teaspoon finely shredded lime peel
1 tablespoon lime juice
1 tablespoon olive oil
1 tablespoon cider vinegar
½ teaspoon salt
¼ teaspoon ground black pepper

MY FIRST SNAKE!

Oh for crying out loud! What now? Snakes, that's what!

When we first took possession of the cabin, we were so enamored with the natural beauty of the surroundings that we decided to keep it just that way. This included not mowing any grasses down. The wild flowers were delicate and pretty in the "yard" areas. Besides, that meant less work for us.

It was July, our third month at the cabin. It was also the onset of really hot weather. The buzzing, clicking and humming of various insects was intense. So as I'm walking through the tall grasses in the back yard, I thought nothing about the rattling sound I was hearing, other than that it had to be a really big bug. Then I heard it again, closer and louder. I froze and watched as slithering in front of me, sporting a tan skin with black diamonds, was a five-foot-long timber rattler. In my eyes, it was as big around as a loaf of French bread (actually, it was).

I screamed and looked at the house. David was at the window watching and was on his way to the rescue. He grabbed a 2-by-4 chunk of wood to hold the snake down and sent me after a shovel. With my heart racing and blood pounding, I raced right by the shovel leaning against the house. Unable to find the shovel that was in plain sight, I grabbed the splitting maul and headed back to the snake. We bludgeoned it until there was no longer any movement. To really finish it off, David placed a rock over it to keep the carcass from becoming a doggie chew toy. The next morning when we went to check out our prize winning rattlesnake skin, it was gone! When we lifted the rock, there was nothing there. So where did it go….

Our yard care ideas have changed. We have mowed the area around the house ever since. The neighbors have said we should have saved the skin on a snake that large. Some creative person could have turned it into a belt, handbag, or hat band.

Better yet, it was suggested that snake become a part of our menu. It tastes a lot like chicken you know. Or so "they" say. I won't touch it.

If you are experienced in the preparation of rattlesnake, here is a suggestion for you. The following recipe is delicious when prepared with kielbasa or other sausage.

The rattlesnake chef may wish to substitute that meat.

PASTA WITH KIELBASA SAUSAGE (OR RATTLESNAKE) AND VERMOUTH

This recipe is outstanding using the kielbasa. I can't vouch for the rattlesnake rendition. Just how adventuresome are you?

1 small rattlesnake*, skinned, head and rattles removed, meat cut into small pieces; or use one kielbasa cut into one-inch chunks
3 yellow onions, sliced and diced
3 tablespoons olive oil
¼ cup or more of sweet vermouth (you could substitute chicken broth)
1 to 2 cups of sliced mushrooms
1 cup water
1 package of curly noodles, cooked
1 cup or more of cream
1 can cream of chicken soup with mushrooms
1 cup sour cream
1½ cups grated mild white cheese such as Gruyére, Swiss, or Muenster
1 box of frozen peas and mushrooms
Salt and black pepper

Brown meat of choice in the olive oil. Add onions and sauté until caramelized. When meat and onions are nicely browned and leaving crispy bits on the bottom of the pan, stir in the vermouth or chicken broth to deglaze the pan. Let this mixture simmer a few minutes to reduce the liquid. Stir in the mushrooms and 1 cup of water and simmer until the mushrooms are tender. Stir in the box of frozen peas and mushrooms. Mix together the cream, chicken soup and sour cream and stir this mixture into the meat mixture. Salt and pepper to taste. Heat through and stir in the cheese. Ladle over hot noodles.

**Do not cook with rattlesnake unless you are experienced with the necessary precautions required to process this reptile.*

YOU CAN'T DO THIS IN TOWN!

In the summer months, we have bat watch. As dusk approaches, everyone chooses a chair on the deck and we get ready. It doesn't take long before bats fill the sky, feeding on small insects in the air. Sometimes they swoop down to the deck where we are sitting. That is always good for a few squeals. I've not had any fly into the house yet. We make sure that the doors are shut during bat-watch time. Their graceful sky diving is great outdoor fun to watch, but that is as far as it goes for bat appreciation. A great snack for bat watch time is called North Woods Crispies. Munch on this as you watch the bats munch on their crispy flying snacks in the air. Your snack is crisp but will not fly no matter how fermented it gets!

NORTH WOODS CRISPIES

The Official Bat Watch Snack

2 pounds mixed nuts without peanuts
1 box (17½ ounce size) Rice Chex
1 box Cheerios (15 ounce size)
1 box Wheat Chex (19½ ounce size)
2 bags stick pretzels
4 cups corn oil (first take the calories out)
5 tablespoons Worcestershire Sauce
2½ tablespoons garlic salt
2½ tablespoons seasoning salt—your choice

In a doubled, large garbage sack, mix nuts and cereals.

Mix salts and oil. Pour a small amount of mixture in bag. Rotate bag to gently mix. Then pour on more salt/oil mixture and rotate bag again. Continue this procedure until all oil has been blended into the cereal.

Pour mixture evenly into 4 large disposable aluminum baking pans. Now distribute the pretzels evenly among the 4 pans and gently mix them in. Bake at 225 degrees stirring every 15 minutes for 2 hours.

WE WANT TO BBQ!

Let's face it. Cooking something on the barbie in a mountain setting seems much better than cooking in the city. Wafting waves of searing meats in the out-of-doors always start one drooling. At this time, I would like to share with you just one little word of advice. The first and most important step for mountain barbecuing is to always lift the lid and thoroughly examine the equipment prior to lighting. If you rush, and omit this all important step, you may get fresher meat than you want. David frequently finds baby mice or families of chipmunks that have moved in and nested. It only takes them a day or two to discover this motel room with the unmade bed.

New recipe idea: Butter with Bugs
Ingredients: Butter, softened
Assortment of flying insects

Preparation: A simple dish to prepare. The following narrative will give you all necessary information.

Regrettably, one enchanted summer evening, the bats went hungry. As they swooped and dove through the skies looking for something to eat, there were no bugs to be found. How do I know this? Because I ate them. Well, not alone, I had company. Dinner on the deck with friends. The wine was open and the table was set. The heavenly scent of seared and sizzling steaks was wafting from the grill. I set out the butter for the baked potatoes and lit some candles to set the mood for our dinner under the stars. Everything was perfect and we ate with gusto.

As the night cooled off, we finished our wine and moved indoors. One at a time, as we brought plates and serving pieces inside, our eyes got bigger and bigger. None of us knew if we should laugh or throw-up.

The wine bottle was full of gnats. The butter was not yellow. It was a mass of dead, dying, and still fluttering tiny flying insects. Our plates had side orders of the same and so did the silverware. The only light outside was from the candles I had lit and from the stars, so we did not see the uninvited dinner guests (or should I call them surprise entrées). That night we all ingested a little extra protein.

Mushroom hunting in the wild is fun. What better way is there to exercise than to tromp up and down mountain sides in search of the delectable morel, calves brain, shaggy mane, or chanterelle mushrooms? The nutty taste and sometimes chewy texture of these wonders of nature need only to be sautéed in butter. Other embellishments are not necessary.

All of this brings me to just one more dinner story. A group of about eight of us had spent the afternoon mushroom hunting in the Bumping Lake area. We felt we had scored big time by managing to fill a large sack full of morels. Back at camp, while the men sat around the campfire telling stories and soaking up the smoke, the women gathered in the kitchen to clean the mushrooms and prepare dinner.

We excitedly washed, trimmed, and sautéed about half of our day's bounty. Of course we were sipping on a little wine as we worked. The mushrooms were tremendous with our steaks and we heartily congratulated each other on a job well done.

The next morning, sautéing a few more of our wonderful morels to go with omelets sounded like a good idea. As we worked in the light of day, one of the girls noticed that there were little black spots inside the mushrooms when you cut into them. Hmm, I wonder what that is? Oh no! As we focus on the little spots, contemplating their existence, it becomes obvious that they are moving. The more we watch, the more they move. Just what did we eat last night? Worms is what! They were little white worms with tiny black spots on their heads.

The remainder of our delectable find went into the garbage. Omelets don't need mushrooms. That was the last time that I ate a wild mushroom. For some reason, the appeal was gone.

However, the following recipe for flank steak is delicious. If you would like to sauté some mushrooms to accompany it, I recommend purchasing a few at the market!

FLANK STEAK SAUTÉ

Wine Note: A lush, peppery Lemberger is very good with this dish.

1 one-pound flank steak
1 large white onion-sliced in half and then slivered
3 tablespoons olive oil

MARINADE:

1 cup Italian salad dressing
1 tablespoon garlic powder
1 tablespoon fresh rosemary (Rumor has it that dried is just as good—but it's not!)
2 teaspoons fresh thyme or 1 teaspoon dried
¼ cup of your favorite smoke-flavored marinade for beef
Plenty of freshly ground black pepper (to taste). Add salt at time of cooking if desired

Marinate steak early in the day or over-night. Heat oil to hot, almost smoking. Sauté onions until browned and al dente.

Remove onions to ovenproof plate and keep warm in oven. Add more oil to the pan if needed. Heat to high heat. Sprinkle both sides of steak with seasoning of choice, place it in the hot oil and cook unturned for 5-10 minutes until seared and brown. Turn and cook additional 5 minutes until desired doneness. Slice across the grain and serve on platter of onions.

DO YOU SMELL SMOKE?

What is it that draws a man to wood, fire, and smoke? I think it dates back to something primal, very primal. David's favorite feature of the cabin when we first moved in was the wood stove. He loved that stove and couldn't wait to use it. In fact his notation in the journal was "I made our first fire in our wood stove for this year. Not real cold out yet, but the smell of the wood burning and its warmth is very nice."

Well the warmth may be nice, but the smell of a campfire is not nice indoors. It did heat well, I will admit that, but it smoked even better. If a log shifted, the stove smoked. If you opened the door to stoke the fire, the stove smoked. It smoked in the middle of the night because nobody was watching and it could. We smelled like a campfire 24 hours a day. I was not happy.

When I was a little girl, my parents had a coal stove that was named Hershvogal—it was awful. I now had a Hershvogal of my own. Even worse, we quickly discovered that when you bring in logs for the fire, you also bring in all manner of spiders along with the bark and dirt.

On one special night when the house had filled with smoke and awakened me, I opened all of the windows, wrapped up in a blanket, sat on the couch for the remainder of the night, and decided that this mountain woman was moving back to town unless some changes were made. Hershvogal had to go! Either I had a heat source with a thermostat, or Mountain Man slept alone. The decision was made to put in a propane stove.

RECIPE FOR HERSHVOGAL SMOKED WOMAN

(not for the faint of heart)

1 old wood stove
4-5 chunks of dirty and bug enhanced forest logs
2 sheets of rolled up newspaper
25 matches (or more depending on how long it takes to get the fire to light)

Open stove door and let old ashes and chunks of whatever the stuff is that remains from the previous fire fall out onto the floor and make a big mess. Bring in the wood from outside and watch as pine needles and other debris drop all over the floor. Put the logs in the stove. Then carefully roll up the first piece of newspaper, light it and try to get a good draft going by sticking it part way up the chimney. Now, shove the second piece of paper under the logs and light it.

The fire should now be burning nicely so that you can easily see the bugs and spiders flee for their lives out from the open door and onto your floor. Finally the bugs are squashed, the door to the stove is shut and the floor has been swept up. Whew! Mountain Man stands back and enjoys the results of his efforts. After a couple of hours, the room has warmed up a little. This old stove only heats up the room it sits in.

Wrapped in flannel jammies and an extra blanket and wearing heavy socks, I crawl into bed. As the night wears on and the wood chunks burn and shift in the stove, one large piece falls to the front and causes the stove to smoke. We wake up to rooms (plural) filled with smoke. It is mid-winter and I'm sitting by an open window just to breathe. My hair is smoked, my clothing—all of it—is smoked, all towels and linens are smoked, and even my cat smells of smoke.

So now you have the rest of the story. You too can make a smoked woman, but I would not recommend it.

WHERE DO I PUT MY CLOTHES? I DON'T CARE ABOUT YOURS!

The wood stove was not the only thing that we replaced. The cabin had no closets, no pantry and no room for family gatherings. At one end of the kitchen, I had stacked some apple boxes on their sides four deep to hold spices and canned goods. Clothes were hung on some little pegs on the walls in the bedroom. For the most part, we were living out of suitcases. The cabin had been built only as a basic two day get-a-way structure. We had to remodel!

We were into year two up here and it just wasn't fun living the life of a camper every day. With all of the digging for items in boxes and suitcases, I was beginning to feel as if I were standing on my head 24 hours a day. A contractor was hired and we set to work.

The remodel consisted of a pantry, extending the kitchen counter, more cupboards, a great room with 21 foot high vaulted ceilings. There was a knotty pine log stairway that led to the loft which contained an office and sitting area and a small area for closets. Three knotty pine closet-cupboard type things were built and installed in the bedroom. That helped a lot. The hot tub was moved to the rear of the house and we installed a new front door with oval glass that was etched with a large bull elk. This should have been a simple enough project except for one fact. My Dad is a retired building contractor – very much a perfectionist. There was nothing that Rod, our contractor, did that was right in Dad's eyes. They argued every step of the way. I remember one day when Dad had his overalls in a bunch and was waiting for Rod at the bridge when he showed up for work. He told Rod that if he couldn't do the work his way, he couldn't do the work and sent him away. Another day it was Rod's turn. His tool belt was poking him in the butt (I guess) and he invited Dad to step outside and go a round or two. Oh brother! It gets better. After long hours of work and numerous skirmishes with the old man, Rod stopped in at the repair shop one afternoon to go over some of his ideas with David. They also discussed how best to deal with Dad. Rod admitted that Dad had some good ideas also, and that he was going to incorporate them into the schematics of the project. But it was our job to get the monkey off of his back. David agreed. As Rod got into his truck and pulled away, Dad pulled up to the door in his baby blue VW pick-up and marched into David's shop. He had parked at the far end of the parking lot and was waiting for Rod to leave. He wanted us to get rid of Rod and find someone else to finish the work. Of course, that was not an option. Rod was doing a great job for us. Dad did feel better when we informed him that Rod was indeed going to use some of his ideas. The bottom line is that David and I were referees for the duration of the project. I don't know how we all made it through in one piece, but we did. Never again!

I needed comfort food, and my favorite comfort food is pasta. The following is a wonderful meal.

BAKED PASTA SHELLS STUFFED WITH RICOTTA AND VEGETABLES

Serves 4-6

16 jumbo pasta shells
1 tablespoon olive oil
2 tablespoons butter
1 medium onion, finely diced
3 cloves of garlic, minced
2 cups mushrooms, quartered
1 sweet red pepper in ¼-inch dice
1 yellow sweet pepper in ¼-inch dice
1 sweet green pepper in ¼-inch dice
1½ pounds ricotta cheese
1 egg, well beaten
½ cup Parmesan cheese, freshly grated
3 tablespoons fresh basil, finely chopped
4 tablespoons fresh parsley, chopped
½ teaspoon oregano
¼ teaspoon salt
¼ teaspoon white pepper
Bread crumbs
3 cups tomato sauce
Additional Parmesan cheese

Preheat oven to 375 degrees

In a large pot of lightly salted water, cook the pasta shells al dente. Remove with a slotted spoon and immerse in a pot of cold water. Place on a paper towel to dry. Set aside.

Heat the oil and butter in a large saucepan over medium heat, sauté the onion, garlic, and mushrooms. Add the peppers and continue to sauté until they begin to cook, but are still crunchy. Place in a bowl and allow to cool at room temperature.

When the vegetable mixture is cool, add the ricotta, egg, Parmesan, basil, half the parsley, oregano, salt, and white pepper. Mix well. If the mixture is too moist, add a little more Parmesan or bread crumbs or a combination of both until it is firm, but still moist.

Line the bottom of a large baking dish with enough tomato sauce to thinly cover it. Gently stuff the cooked pasta shells with the ricotta mixture and place them in the baking dish side by side. Spoon a little sauce over each shell and sprinkle with Parmesan cheese.

Bake the shells for about 30 minutes or until the sauce is bubbling and the cheese mixture is hot. Let stand for 10-15 minutes and serve with additional Parmesan cheese.

WE WILL NEVER FORGET...

Our first early evenings at the cabin were spent just sitting on the deck and watching the critters run across the steep mountain side behind our home. At first glance the area seemed empty except for the trees and other forms of vegetation. However, as you sit quietly, everything comes to life with animal and bird activity. We would sit for hours, just staring straight ahead and not saying a word. The newness and epic changes in our life had us wrapped around its little finger.

Many nights have also been spent around the campfire telling stories in the dark, with only the light from the fire. Of course everyone has their own stick to poke at the fire with and make the red embers glow even more. The elk can be heard crashing through the brush and the deer come in to feed. There are extended quiet times when each and every one of us are deep in our own thoughts about the wonder of living here.

Campfires tend to bring out all kinds of interesting secrets. One particular favorite of mine was when we learned that our grandson, Mike, kept imaginary dancing girls under his bed and in a box in his closet. As you can imagine, the more we laughed, the more he giggled and the more stories came out. It was amazing the amount of dancing girls one 5-year-old little boy could get into a closet and still shut the door.

Granddaughter ,Alexis, loved to roast marshmallows. For her, they weren't done until they were almost burnt, droopy, saggy and sticky to the point of almost falling off of the stick. I love them that way too. We fashioned special sticks for roasting at the campfire. My Dad fixed up some dandies. He cut off shovel and rake handles and then fastened fabricated metal 6-inch forks to the end of each one. They worked great and kept the hot dogs from falling off the wimpy willow sticks we had been using. The only problem was that we could never find a shovel, rake or hoe with a handle on it. They had all been used for the roasting utensils.

One last helpful hint for around the campfire: if you sit with your feet propped up on the surrounding rocks and are not careful, the soles of your shoes will melt and flop off!

You just haven't lived unless you have experienced the dynamite taste of a hot dog, slightly charred over the campfire (just a little black & crispy), with mustard, relish, ketchup, and a scoop of caramelized sweet onions all piled into a hotdog bun. WOW & WONDERFUL!

Now for desert. Build a s'more North Woods style.

NORTH WOODS S'MORES
OR
SHOE SOLE FLAMBÉ

Graham crackers
Marshmallows
Chocolate candy bars (with or without nuts). I like nuts.

The rules are simple.

First, place two marshmallows on the roasting fork that has been fabricated by your grandfather.

Then cook the marshmallow to your preferred degree of doneness. The gooier the better as far as I'm concerned. Then snap a graham cracker in half, lay a chunk of chocolate bar on the graham cracker, top this with a hot, flame-cooked, ooey-gooey, slightly charred marshmallow and lastly, top with the other half of graham cracker.

Smoosh this wonderful sandwich together and take the biggest bite you can. It truly doesn't get any better than this.

Then you can grin at your campfire circle neighbor, with chocolaty teeth and sticky marshmallow running down your face and look at everyone who is doing the same thing.

THE SUMMER FORT

As with most children, Alexis and Mike have unending imagination and love to be creative outside. It didn't take them long to discover a huge fir tree in the front of the cabin that had long draping branches which formed a fair sized room that they called the Summer Fort. It was quickly filled up with wagons, trucks, toys, buckets and shovels, plastic rakes, little cars, and a flat board to hold their lunch. The routine upon arrival at the cabin was to run upstairs, put on their hats (so ticks couldn't get in their hair) and head for the fort.

After the first snow, I watched wagon loads of toys and the board for lunch being dragged around to the back of the house. Curious, I said, "Watcha doing?" The prompt reply was that they were moving to the Winter Fort.

Silly me. I hadn't realized that there was room for rent in the back yard! The winter fort evergreen had much longer branches which created a much more spacious play area and room to plan the next expedition. Snowflakes did not pass through the thick branches of the winter fort so the floor of this room stayed frozen but dry. It did, however, take about a half hour to prepare the children for the excursion from the back door to the opening of the fort.

Depending on the day, there could be from two to four feet or more of snow on the ground. These weather conditions necessitated the donning of snowsuits, hats, mittens, scarves, two pairs of socks, and boots. Just when you thought they were ready to head out the door, one of them would announce, "I have to go potty." It only takes once or twice for this to happen and then you remember to ask prior to dressing.

Adventurers do get hungry. What fun is it if you are exploring with nothing to eat? A favorite is peanut butter and jelly sandwiches and hot chocolate.

PB & J FOR THE NORTH WOODS FORT DWELLER

4 slices soft white bread crust removed as the kids will not eat it anyway
Feed the crust to the birds
Jar of peanut butter
1 large spoon to scoop generous helpings of peanut butter onto bread
1 jar of strawberry jam
1 cookie cutter in a tree shape

First cut the bread into tree shapes. Then spread peanut butter onto one side of a tree. Spread jam on one side of another tree. Place jam and peanut butter trees together. Serve with tall glasses of milk or mugs of hot chocolate depending on the season. Serves two hungry fort dwellers. If you are lucky you will be invited to join them!

WE'RE SO PROUD!

I am very proud of my grandchildren. My husband, David, is proud of them too and we love having them around. However, I have learned that men and women can be proud of children for different reasons.

On a particularly hot Saturday afternoon David and Mike and I were down at the river, throwing rocks and splashing around. Alexis was there too, but just a little further downstream investigating some bugs under a rock.

Mike announced that he had to pee. He didn't hesitate to drop his drawers, lean back a little, and let it fly. Grandpa watched with his mouth hung open and chin resting on his chest in total disbelief. "WOW! Has that boy got pressure!" Grandpa is so proud.

Whatever. ....

MICHAEL'S FAVORITE PINK FROSTED SHORTBREAD COOKIES (TOOKIES)

"Oh tay, Dramma! – That's it, jus' one more tookie," three-year-old Michael said defiantly as he stood up from his perch on the bottom step of the stairway that lead to the sleeping loft of the cabin. He marched determinedly over to the kitchen counter that held the prized pink frosted shortbread cookies and chose the largest one. There are never enough 'tookies' for Mikie!

When I was catering for the Nordstrom store in Yakima, they ordered 18 dozen three-inch by four-inch cookies a week. It was the favorite cookie that I did for them. That is a lot of pink cookies!

1 cup of butter
½ cup granulated sugar
2½ cups sifted all-purpose flour

Cream the butter and sugar until light and fluffy. Stir in the flour. Pat dough onto an ungreased cookie sheet, forming a rectangle. For a melt-in-your mouth cookie, the dough should be about ½-inch thick or slightly less. With a fork prick the dough to create a square, rectangular or diamond pattern all over the top depending. This will determine what shape and size you want your cookies to be.

Bake in 300 degree oven about 30 minutes. Cookies should be set but not browned at all. Remove from oven and cut the cookies along the lines made by the fork. Remove from cookie sheet and cool on wire rack. Frost with cream cheese frosting.

PINK FROSTING:

1 (3-ounce) package cream cheese, softened
1 tablespoon butter softened
1 teaspoon vanilla
Dash salt
2 cups confectioner's sugar
Pink food coloring

Combine cream cheese, butter and vanilla. Beat at low speed until light and smooth. Gradually add sugar and salt. Beat until fluffy. If necessary, add milk to make a spreading consistency. Color lightly with a few drops of food coloring.

THE WHIZZER'S LEMONADE
— OR —
OLD-FASHIONED LEMON BALM LEMONADE

4 large juicy lemons, washed and scrubbed
2/3 cup granulated sugar
1 1/4 quarts cold water
A bunch of fresh balm leaves
Ice cubes

Peel the lemons and put the lemon peels into a large heatproof pitcher. Add the sugar and pour on enough boiling water to dissolve the sugar. Add half the fresh balm leaves. Leave to infuse until completely cool. When cool, squeeze the juice from the lemons and add to the syrup. Pour in the cold water to taste, adjusting the sugar or lemon juice to get a good balance. Chill for about 2 hours. Just before serving, remove the balm and add more fresh sprigs of the herb and ice cubes. At this point you may also like to remove the lemon peel; if the peel is left in the liquid for too long, it can become bitter.

Lemon balm grows easily in the north woods as does mint. They are in the same family. The lemon flavor of balm is much more delicate than that of lemon verbena, so it can be used in large quantities for vegetable and fruit salads. An oil and vinegar dressing will greatly benefit from a handful of the chopped leaves. The gentle taste of the fresh leaves also combines well with all kinds of fruit, so experiment with the whole leaves as a garnish, or chop the leaves and add to fresh fruit salads or fruit fillings for pies and baked desserts. The leaves are also suitable for use in stuffings, and to flavor jams, jellies and sorbets. They are delicious when used to reinforce the flavor in a lemon mousse.

The fresh leaves are often used for cooling drinks, and tisanes. In France, the tea called melissa tea is taken as a tonic and remedy for tiredness. In the Middle East, the herb is used to make a fragrant and refreshing hot drink, in much the same way that mint is used. The herb is a wonderful addition to fruit drinks and wine punches, or homemade lemonade. Both children and adults will enjoy the refreshing taste of lemon balm lemonade, and the beverages authentically sweet rather than over-sweet like many commercial types of lemonade.

NAP TIME? WELL, MAYBE NOT

Picture this: a huge hammock made of comfortable cotton roping complete with a drink holder, a fluffy pillow, and a good book. The hammock is secured at each end to tall, majestic fir trees whose branches are gently whispering in the breeze. The sound of the river flowing nearby is a lullaby for the senses. Could this idyllic setting have a hazard?

Yes it can! Almost asleep, you are barely aware that the wind has picked up. It has been a hot day and the extra air movement feels good against your skin. So you just relax and enjoy the afternoon.

CRACK!

Now your eyes are open, wide open as you watch a large section of dead tree branch coming straight toward you as if the tree was harpooning you for screwing the hammock hooks into its trunk. The force of the wind has snapped the dead branch loose and all you can do is watch it come. Fortunately, that same wind has one more gust in it that carries the branch just to the right of the hammock, where it buries itself vertically into the ground about six inches.

Now, it is not unusual for the wind to knock loose, old, dead branches from trees. The trick is not to be underneath these falling missiles. My second close encounter was on a lovely day in June. I was working in the garden when gale force winds suddenly came up. I heard the cracking from above and just had time to put my arms over my head for protection and hope for the best.

The branch that came crashing to ground was approximately eight feet long and six inches in diameter. It landed on one of Dad's prize blueberry bushes and destroyed a large portion of it. The good news is that it missed me. The blueberry bush will never be the same but it will grow more branches.

The blueberry bushes were in their second season and doing quite well. When Mom and Dad made the move to this mountain country from the low lands of Wapato, the twenty-one blueberry bushes from Dad's garden had to come along also. Everyone said that blueberries wouldn't grow in the mountains, but he proved them wrong!

Blueberries, fresh or frozen, make great muffins.

NORTH WOODS BLUEBERRY STREUSEL MUFFINS

6 Large Muffins

1¾ cups all-purpose flour
½ cup sugar
2¾ teaspoons baking powder
2 teaspoons grated lemon rind
¾ teaspoon salt
1 egg, slightly beaten
¾ cup milk
1/3 cup vegetable oil
1 cup fresh or frozen blueberries*
1 tablespoon all-purpose flour
1 tablespoon sugar
¼ cup sugar
2½ tablespoons butter
½ teaspoons ground cinnamon
1½ tablespoons butter

Combine first 5 dry ingredients in a large bowl; make a well in center of mixture. Combine egg, milk, and vegetable oil; stir well. Add to dry ingredients, stirring just until moistened.

Combine blueberries, 1 tablespoon flour, and 1 tablespoon sugar, tossing gently to coat. Fold blueberry mixture into batter. Spoon batter into 6 large (3½-inch) greased muffin pans or lined with paper muffins pans, filling two-thirds full.

TOPPING: Combine ¼ cup sugar with ½ teaspoon cinnamon. Cut in 2½ tablespoons butter with a pastry blender until mixture resembles coarse meal.

Sprinkle over batter. Bake at 400 degrees for 20-25 minutes or until golden. Remove from pans immediately.

Note: If using frozen berries, do not thaw them. Stir frozen berries directly into the flour-sugar mixture and then into the batter.

WHY DID THE FOLKS JOIN US IN THE MOUNTAINS?

The basic truth is that they had nowhere else to go. They were both getting on in age and their home in Wapato, the surrounding grounds and garden were just too much for them to manage. It was not until Mom had her first stroke that they were willing to admit that a change had to be made. Dad thought that Mom had been acting differently but he didn't know what to do about it. For instance, she would get up at midnight and put a roast in the oven for dinner. This is not the normal time frame for meal preparation. She had had a stroke.

We were about a two-hour drive away from them. I was the only one available to help care for them so David and I came up with a care plan. In the morning I would help to open the auto repair shop. Then, there was a trip to the market to do grocery shopping for the folks. The drive to Wapato gave me some extra "think time" so that was OK. I can always use that. Once there, I did the laundry, some house cleaning, prepared meals, assisted with Mom's physical therapy, dispensed medication and whatever was required. Then, the drive back to Selah to pick up David and head for home. By the time we fed the dog, had dinner, did a load of wash and gave the cat a pet or two, it was time for bed. As days ran into weeks, this schedule became increasingly difficult.

When the green house (now my gift shop) at the end of the lane came up for sale, we knew what we had to do. We invited the folks to come and live in the mountains and be our neighbors. At first they were excited about it, but worried about living so far from town. Dad gave it some more thought and said they would not make the move. He had always wanted to live in the mountains, but they would not come. So David wrote them a very moving and heartfelt letter. In that letter, he told them how much he loved them and wanted them to come and live by us. It was two pages long. The next day I read them the letter (David couldn't leave the shop. He had to work). I had tears in my eyes before I had finished page one. The letter had touched their hearts also and the decision was made to move.

We completed the purchase of the green house, and I began packing up a house with an accumulation of 35 years of stuff and memories. It took me about two weeks to pack up and clean up the place. This was a very sad time in my life. Helping elderly parents is all part of the circle of life and all families deal with it, but somehow that knowledge didn't help. They moved to their new home in the fall of 2002 shortly before Thanksgiving. From then on they were referred to affectionately as "The Neighbors". I was able to watch over them during the week and every Sunday was a special dinner to share with them. Saturday morning was guy time and Dad would walk down the lane to have coffee with David and solve the world's problems. The blueberries were transplanted in the spring of the following year.

Parents and blueberries did well under our care for four years. Increasing health care demands for both of them finally necessitated a move to an assisted living facility. The blueberries are still here and loving it. We were told that blueberries wouldn't grow in our mountain soil – think again. We start picking berries in July and don't finish until October's frost is on the ground. Berries by the dozens make their way into baking pans and jam jars. Hundreds go into the freezer. I've learned that mosquitoes also hang out in the blueberries. Mattie loves blueberries too. The berries are a great reason to have blue teeth. During the peak of the season, I'm inviting friends and neighbors to "Come and help yourself." Please. Actually, I have found that the blueberry patch is a great place to hide out. The bushes are approximately six-feet tall and no one can see me and my wine glass, oh, and the berry bucket of course, "working all alone".

One of their favorite meals was meatloaf and mashed potatoes. Dad even learned how to make meatloaf. Here is the recipe for Glenn's meatloaf. I like mine with lots of ketchup.

GLENN'S SAUSAGE MEATLOAF

Dad says: "To make bread crumbs, dry bread, break it up, and crush it with a rolling pin. If you use a knife, the bread flies everywhere."

2 eggs
¾ cup milk
1 pound hamburger
1 pound mild Italian sausage
4 cloves garlic, minced
½ large onion, chopped
1 teaspoon ground sage
1 cup dried bread crumbs
2 tablespoons parsley
1 teaspoon salt
1 teaspoon dry mustard
1 teaspoon black pepper

Combine eggs, milk, bread crumbs, onions, garlic, parsley, salt pepper, dry mustard and sage. Add beef and sausage and mix well. Pat into a greased baking pan. Bake 350 degrees for about 1 hour or until browned and cooked through. Drain grease from pan.

I like mine really brown, almost black, and crispy on top and bottom. Dad also says: "Be sure to use a fork to eat with because fingers are messy."

THE BOMBING BEGINS

In the months of August and September we have another pine tree related event. As the farmers and orchardists are harvesting their crops so too are the Douglas squirrels. These cute, brown, furry animals with tan tummies and big fluffy tails are diligent and hard workers. They can cut pinecones out of a tree faster than you could pick apples. The sound the falling cones make when striking a metal roof is resonating.

It was soccer tournament time again. In mid-August our son's soccer team makes their annual trek from Seattle to play in the Yakima Sunburn tournament and stay the weekend with us. As usual, some of them were spending the night in our motorhome, which was parked under the trees. It just happened also to be a pinecone harvesting weekend. Our guests needed to be up early to make game time. However, there was no need to set the alarm clock.

The squirrels, early risers that they are, began work about 5:00 a.m. I was at the kitchen in the beginning stages of breakfast preparation when I heard the first cones hit.

Bang! Bang! Bang!

The pinecone bombing had begun. The cones were landing just seconds apart and striking the motorhome roof with force. I watched and waited knowing that soon Mother Nature would have everyone up for the day. It didn't take long. As the young people emerged from the motorhome still half asleep, looking around, rubbing their heads and obviously puzzled by the noise, the bombing continued. The squirrels were relentless. Pine cones were dropping everywhere. The ground was covered. The squirrels with their little paws and faces covered with pitch from the cones were hard at it. I just enjoyed the show.

Ron's visit with his soccer team is a highly anticipated and much enjoyed highlight of our year. The weather is usually hot, hot, hot! The natural thing to do after a soccer game is to grab towels, swim suits, beverages and hit the river.

The sunny side of the river was lined with relaxing soccer players. David was taking pictures from the bridge and I was on the other side of the river in a more shady spot with a glass of Chardonnay. It is always so fun to watch them having such a great time. The river was cold but refreshing.

There is no better ending to a long Northwest summer day than a backyard barbecue with a finale of luscious berry shortcake, especially if you have picked the berries yourself. The Northwest has a large variety of wild berries, from blackberries to tiny purple huckleberries.

NORTH WOODS BERRY SHORTCAKE

BERRIES:

4 cups (1 ½ pounds) fresh berries in season, such as strawberries, raspberries, blueberries or blackberries
¼-½ cup sugar, depending on the tartness of the berries
2 tablespoons berry liqueur (optional)

SHORTCAKE:

2 cups all-purpose flour
2 ½ teaspoons baking powder
1 teaspoon salt
¼ cup sugar
1/3 cup vegetable shortening
¼ cup sliced almonds, lightly toasted
¾-1 cup whole milk (2% works ok too)

WHIPPING CREAM:

1 cup heavy cream
1/3 cup sifted powdered sugar
2 tablespoons amaretto liqueur
Fresh mint sprigs (optional)
Mild tasting edible flowers*, such as johnny-jump-ups (optional)

Preheat an oven to 375 degrees. In a large bowl, lightly toss the berries with the sugar, add liqueur. Chill for about an hour.

Make the shortcake: into a large bowl, sift together the flour, baking powder, salt and sugar. Cut in the shortening with a pastry cutter. Then stir in the nuts. Lightly stir in as much milk as is needed to make a soft, moist dough.

Turn the dough out onto a lightly floured surface. Lightly pat the dough to ½ inch thick. Cut the dough into 1½-inch rounds with a biscuit cutter. Place the biscuits, sides touching, on a baking sheet.

Bake the biscuits in the preheated oven about 18-20 minutes or until they are lightly browned. Let cool.

Right before serving, whip the cream in a deep bowl until soft peaks form. Whisk in the powdered sugar and liqueur, and a spoonful of berry juice, if desired. Split the biscuits in half crosswise.

On each of 6 large chilled plates, place a split biscuit bottom, spoon berries over it and top with a dollop of whipped cream. Place the biscuit top on slightly askew. Garnish with mint sprigs, if you like.

Dust the rims of the plates with powdered sugar shaken from a sieve.

For the ultimate presentation, top off with edible flowers.

**Be sure that the flowers have not been sprayed with pesticide. Nor should they come from a florist.*

THE LOCALS

Lacking shopping malls and movie theaters, we get our entertainment by watching the locals—local animals, that is. For the most part, the animal adventures have been outside. But if you forget to shut the door, surprises await.

It was a Friday afternoon and I was working downtown. Our son, Ron, had come over to the cabin early with the kids, Michael and Alexis. He phoned me at work to check in and find out what was for dinner. As we visited, suddenly he went quiet. Then I heard "OH OH", silence, "OH NO", silence, and then "Okay".

I'm yelling at the receiver in my hand "What, what, what?" Turns out an over-friendly chipmunk had run through the open door, circled the kitchen a couple of times and then ran back outside. This city boy from Seattle thought for awhile he would be chasing that chipmunk around the house with a net and was very relieved when it ran back outside.

Our neighbors had a deer walk into their house that didn't want to leave. I'd rather chase the chipmunk.

I never go barefoot if the house is dark and I cannot see the floor. This lesson was learned the first week at the cabin. My cat, Corky, a short haired gray and white tabby, weighs in at 27 pounds. She is a full-time inside cat. I expect her to defend and protect me from all invasive rodents. She does her job. There has only been one mouse in the house. The slaying took place in the wee hours of the night when all was dark. There were no stars or moonlight shining in through the windows. All was black.

Sometime after the slaying, nature called to me. As I paddled to the bathroom in my bare feet, guess what I stepped on? My fat cat was just too well-fed and couldn't be bothered to skin and de-bone her own meal. Her gourmet treats must come out of a little foil pouch from Purina that says "Tear Here" on it. At any rate, the murder victim was underneath my big toe and it was still warm. This is why Mountain Woman wears shoes. It is not because she doesn't want to get her feet dirty!!

Louisa and her husband, Jim, live at the end of the lane. She is a retired marine biologist and researcher from the University of Washington. They have made Deer Cove their home for the past 15 years. It's like having a nature encyclopedia for a neighbor. I frequently call on her with questions. She always has an answer for me and sometimes a chuckle for herself, at my expense.

A little summer yard work had me outside hard at it when I started hearing a knocking noise. It happened again and again. Putting my shovel down, I started looking around. It didn't take long to spot a rather large, white bird on the side of a big fir tree. It was pecking like a woodpecker and it looked like a woodpecker but I expected all woodpeckers to be red and black. I went inside and called Louisa. As it turns out, there is such a thing as a white woodpecker. It is very rare and I was privileged to see it.

I have indeed learned that you can't fight Mother Nature. Instead, pay attention, let her teach you and learn to love what she has to offer. The following recipe is fun to make and fun to serve at parties as an appetizer.

MARY'S MICE COOKIES

(You can thank Corky for this recipe.)
Yield: 1½ dozen mice!

2/3 cup semisweet chocolate chips
2 cups chocolate wafer crumbs (about 40 wafers), divided
1/3 cup sour cream
36 red nonpareils
¼ cup sliced almonds
18 pieces black shoestring licorice (2 inches each)

In a microwave-safe bowl, melt chocolate chips; stir until smooth. Stir in 1 cup of crumbs and sour cream. Cover and refrigerate for 1 hour or until easy to handle.

For each mouse, roll about 1 tablespoon chocolate mixture into a ball, tapering one end to resemble a mouse. Roll in remaining chocolate crumbs to coat. Position nonpareils for eyes, almond slices for ears and licorice pieces for tails.

PECAN SHORTBREAD COOKIES

This recipe is a bonus and only in here because I like it.

¾ cup butter, softened
½ cup confectioner's sugar
2 cups all-purpose flour
½ teaspoon salt

FILLING:
2 squares (1 ounce each) unsweetened chocolate
4 eggs
1½ cups packed brown sugar
2 teaspoons vanilla extract
1 cup finely chopped pecans

In a large mixing bowl, cream butter and confectioner's sugar until light and fluffy. Combine flour and salt; gradually add to creamed mixture and mix well. Press into an ungreased 15-in.x10-in.x1-in. baking pan.

Bake at 375 degrees for 12-15 minutes or until lightly browned. Cool for 5 minutes on a wire rack. Reduce temperature to 350 degrees.

To make filling, in a microwave safe bowl, melt chocolate; stir until smooth. Cool. In a large bowl, combine the eggs, brown sugar, vanilla, salt and melted chocolate; fold in pecans. Pour filling over crust. Bake for 18 to 20 minutes or until filling is set. Cool completely on a wire rack. Cut into diamond-shaped bars. Yield: 5 dozen.

THE SILVER FUR COAT!

Could it be a fur coat in the making—maybe? The ground in our area is incredibly porous. It contains lots of sand and fine rock along with the boulders. Summer watering is difficult so David rented a ditch digging device and put in an underground sprinkler system. It was during the time that our yard was full of trenches in preparation for the sprinkler pipes that I saw it—silver fur running down the trenches. Holy smokes was it a gorgeous thing! Its little head would pop up from the trench, look around, and away he would go again. I just had to stand there at the window and watch.

The tail was big and fluffy and the fur formed a white chevron shape over the back of the shoulder blade area. I knew it had to be an ermine. I've seen fur coats that look like this beauty. I called Louisa. She laughed. My ermine turned out to be a California gray squirrel. They are often referred to as gray diggers.

Louisa informed me that they eat everything and anything plant wise. I have a friend who likes squirrel soup and thought about calling him. It was just a thought. I did not call. The squirrel was too pretty. I was hoping that it would selectively eat the weeds and leave my flowers alone.

Now we know that gray diggers won't leave anything alone. We also know that they are good at making more gray diggers. One year we had 5 and the next year we had 40. My friend and neighbor, Lynda, has a live trap that we have borrowed. These squirrels have a sincere fondness for apples. With Lynda's trap and a few apples, we have successfully trapped and relocated all of them. We hope. If not, then I've got more apples. Dad's pies might be a little shorted, but the sacrifice is worth it.

Helpful Mattie, our dog, had quite a trapping system of her own and proudly brought Ronnie and I a gray squirrel one sunny afternoon. She had her feelings hurt and crushed to the ground when we scolded her. We had to proceed with a water burial and floated the squirrel down the river. To date, Mattie has not trapped another squirrel.

Normally, I was the one to call Louisa but on one fall afternoon she called me with a warning. From our cabin it is a short walk to get the mail and paper. A pine needle covered lane leads to a wood planked bridge that crosses the Naches river. The mail and paper receptacles are across the road. It is a pleasant walk, a chance to stretch your legs and breathe in some of the fresh mountain air. Unless you are greeted by an angry three-point white tailed buck.

That afternoon Louisa had gone for her mail and was coming back across the bridge with her hands full when this buck with an attitude started to cross from the other side. For some reason, he had his knickers in a knot and had decided not to let Louisa pass by. As he lowered his head and charged at her, she dropped the mail and grabbed onto his antlers. This quick action was enough to defray the force of his charge. Luckily, he only made one run at her. Louisa was shaken up, her pants were torn, and her leg had a long gash.

Her ability to act in the face of imminent danger probably saved her life. That has been the only bad experience that we have had with deer to date.

Even though I decided not to invite my friend to come hunting squirrels for soup, I do have a great recipe.

SQUIRREL SOUP
OTHERWISE KNOWN AS
MARY'S FAMOUS POT ROAST SOUP

1 pot roast (2 to 3-pound) or 3 large squirrels
3 bay leaves
2 tablespoons dried spaghetti seasoning
2 cups ketchup
1 cup macaroni
2 cups red potatoes, cubed and not peeled
2 carrots, peeled and sliced
2 stalks of celery sliced
1 cup green beans—frozen or fresh
1 red sweet bell pepper—chopped
1 cup sweet peas
1 large onion—chopped
6 or more cups water
1½ teaspoons salt, optional
1 teaspoon black pepper
2 teaspoons dried sage
1 tablespoon dried basil
¼ cup fresh basil
¼ cup fresh parsley

Brown pot roast on medium-high heat on both sides. Add water and bay leaves. Place in 375 oven and cook until tender, about 2-3 hours.

Remove meat and transfer to cutting board. Strain juices. Trim all fat from meat and cut into small chunks. Chill broth to set fat and skim fat off. Add remaining ingredients to broth except pasta and add water if necessary to cover.

Simmer about 30 minutes. Add pasta. Continue cooking until veggies and pasta are tender. Stir in meat chunks. Adjust seasoning–salt and pepper as needed to taste. Serve with salad, bread and cheese.

YUMMY! YUMMY!

THE CHICKEN RACE

"From There To Here, From Here To There, Funny Things Are Everywhere."
— Dr. Seuss

Mountain people are so easily entertained. Move over, honey, here comes the chicken! Our neighbor, Lynda, has a chicken named Henny Penny. David, Ron, Michael, Alexis and I were on a Sunday afternoon walk. Our dogs were with us. We were just soaking up the sun, chatting and enjoying being together when Henny Penny came into view.

The dogs saw her first and the race was on! Michael and Alexis started jumping up and down, laughing and screaming. David took off on a dead run to the right of the house, yelling at the dogs to come back. The dogs at this point are "deaf." Ron takes off to the left in hopes of grabbing the chicken. Michael and Alexis are still jumping and squealing up a storm.

This is just too much excitement for me. All I can do is stand there and watch and hope I don't have to start taping feathers back on a chicken. The first to show was the chicken bursting through the bushes, feathers flying, but still intact. Ron missed his chance to grab it. The dogs tied for second place with David a close third. Ron didn't place because he ran the wrong way. The kids were still jumping and laughing. I was watching for the neighbor and hoping that I wouldn't have to explain why my crazy family was running circles around her house. It was the chicken race of the century.

Needless to say, this chicken was mad and hot as hell, which reminded me of a great way to cook a bird like this so that the dogs would not be tempted to chase it again.

We could, in fact, be saving the EMT'S a trip up the mountain to resuscitate a chicken having a stroke or a heart attack. Here's the recipe.

By the way, we did not eat Henny Penny.

HOT-AS-HELL CHICKEN

INGREDIENTS FOR PEANUT SAUCE:

- 2 teaspoons peeled, chopped fresh ginger
- 2 teaspoons chopped cilantro
- 2 cloves garlic
- 2 fresh jalapeño peppers
- ½ cup red wine vinegar
- ½ cup soy sauce
- 1 heaping cup of creamy peanut butter*
- 2 teaspoons curry powder, toasted‡
- ¼ cups honey
- 2 teaspoons dark sesame oil

‡To toast the curry powder: sprinkle it in a Teflon® lined sauté pan, use a spatula to stir it constantly over medium heat for just a few seconds to release it's aroma and enhance the flavor.

INGREDIENTS FOR CHICKEN:

- 1 tablespoon olive oil
- 4 (6-ounce) chicken breast halves
- ½ cup dry sherry
- 1 cup sweet hot chili sauce
- ½ pound dried Chinese egg noodles cooked al dente and tossed with a dash of vegetable oil
- ½ cup dry-roasted peanuts or cashews for garnish-optional
- 3-4 green onions, minced for garnish-optional

To prepare the peanut sauce, combine the ginger, cilantro, garlic, jalapeño, vinegar, soy sauce, and peanut butter in the bowl of a food processor and process until smooth. Scrape down the sides of the bowl and add the curry powder, honey, and sesame oil. Process until smooth. Set aside.

Meanwhile, in a very large sauté pan, heat the oil over high heat until smoking hot. Put the chicken breasts in the pan and brown them well about 2 minutes on each side. Decrease the heat to medium and cook for another 2-3 minutes. Add the sherry, increase the heat to high and cook until about half of the sherry remains, 2-3 minutes. Add the chili sauce and turn the breasts to coat them well. Decrease the heat to low and slowly simmer while you prepare the noodles. Put the noodles a large pot of boiling water and cook for 2 minutes to heat through. Strain the noodles and place in a large bowl. Toss them with half of the peanut sauce and place on a serving platter. Remove the chicken breast from the sauce and slice. Place the chicken slices on the noodles and pour some of the remaining sauce over the top. Sprinkle with the roasted peanuts and scallions. Serve hot.

Note: If you don't care for peanuts or can't eat them due to an allergy, substitute 1 cup of North Woods Habañero Peach Marmalade for the peanut butter and eliminate the nuts for the garnish. This recipe makes a ton of sauce.

North Woods Habañero Peach Marmalade is available at *www.MarysPlaceGifts.com*. Orange marmalade could also be used. For the "heat," add ¼ teaspoon of minced habañero peppers. Use this pepper with caution. It is very hot and not kind to your skin. I suggest wearing gloves when handling them. Above all, do not rub your eyes or any part of your face.

GIANT CHICKENS?

There have been a few nice days when I would take my paperwork outside. On a quiet, peaceful afternoon you can get a lot done as long as the wind doesn't decide to blow and do your filing for you. This particular afternoon was very still, until strange sounds started coming from the nearby underbrush.

I didn't know what to expect. The animal trouncing through the thick growth of vegetation sounded big. There was a lot of rustling and loud thrashing noise headed my way. The animals that finally emerged and came strutting into view turned out to be three of the biggest chickens or smallest turkeys I'd ever seen. As I sat there, they paraded in front of me with their tails fanned out. They moved slowly and deliberately across the grassy area just in front of the deck that I was working on. My presence did not bother them.

When they had gone, I looked for them in my Audubon bird book to try and identify them. The afternoon visitors had been sharp-tailed grouse. I have been told that these are really dumb birds. If a hunter fires a shot at a grouse that is sitting on a tree, and misses, the bird will wait for him to take another shot. Not a very bright thing to do.

David and I came home from work one summer afternoon and found two dead grouse lying under a window. Obviously one grouse had flown into the window hard enough to snap its neck so the second one did too! These are known as kamikaze birds.

Now, if you are lucky enough to have fresh grouse handed to you, and you can beat the black lab and the stray cat to these North Woods delicacies, this is what you do. What a treat you will have!

WINDOW-KILL GROUSE WITH PAN GRAVY AND WILD MUSHROOMS
— OR —
GROUSE A LA CRÈME

1 grouse (3-3½ pounds) cut into quarters (discard legs)
1½ cups flour seasoned with salt and pepper
1 cup vegetable oil
1 cup chicken stock
2 tablespoons minced shallots
1½ pints heavy cream
3 ounces (6 tablespoons) cream sherry
3 ounces (6 tablespoons) white wine
1 teaspoon salt
Salt and pepper to taste
1 pound mushrooms of choice, sliced

Roll grouse in flour and brown in skillet in hot oil. Drain.

Place grouse in a casserole dish. Add chicken stock and shallots. Cover and bake at 350 degrees for 1½ hours. Add cream, sherry, white wine and 1 teaspoon salt and the mushrooms. Continue baking until grouse is tender and sauce is thick, about another 1½ hours. (You must use cream to get the sauce to thicken. Do not substitute.) Season to taste with salt and pepper.

HINT: The secret to cooking moist, tender grouse is to cook it in chicken stock, covered, over moderate heat for a long period of time. Pheasant and chicken can be prepared in this same manner.

NO ROSE PARADE FOR ME!

We have quite a parade of animals and birds to share the wilderness with. To accompany that parade many of them make their own music. The grouse are drummers. In the early morning hours you can hear the definite drumming sounds as the birds beat their wings against their bodies.

The elk are the buglers. Their melody is piercing and haunting. We mostly hear this in the evening and early morning. If we could only orchestrate the chirping crickets, croaking frogs, buzzing bees, and mosquitoes, the chirp type bark of the squirrels and the many varied songs of the enchanting birds, what a captivating recording we would have. Round it off with the drummers and buglers and a background of wind and rushing river for a true north woods sound spectacular.

Despite the lovely outdoor symphony, animals are not the best garden guests. You can keep out the deer and the elk with fences, but not the mice.

I planted roses and watched them grow some beautiful blooms. After selecting just the right crystal bowl in which to float a lovely flower, I headed for the garden with shears in hand. I gently grasped the perfect bloom, raised it slightly for snipping, and the entire bush fell over. The eight foot fence around the garden had successfully stopped the large animals from feasting on my plants. So why did my roses die? The mice had eaten the roots, every one. No rose petals for me this year.

But I do have a chocolate lily. It was a surprise find one day when I was mowing the grass in the orchard portion of the garden. They are quite rare and I was excited. Unfortunately, by the time I saw it, the lawn mower had spotted it also and chopped off its little head. There is now a small stake in the ground by the lily and it comes back every year with more blooms.

I have mushrooms as well hiding in the grass. My varieties are morels, shaggy manes, and Prince something or other. Something that does not hide in the grass, however, is mint. I grow several varieties. They have adapted well in the North Woods.

There is a trick to growing mint.

Prepare your soil, make a small hole for the plant, place the plant start in the hole, add water and quickly jump back and out of the way. That is how fast mint will grow. One reason for growing the mint is to have it on hand fresh for Tandoori Chicken Salad.

TANDOORI CHICKEN SALAD

I like to drizzle a zesty Italian salad dressing over the top. Sometimes for variation, I will toast the naan bread, cut it into quarters, and place the wedges decoratively on top of the salad.

Serves 4

4 large naan breads (or pappadams—they are hard to find)
½ cup rice
1 teaspoon tumeric powder
1 fresh mango seeded and sliced
2 tomatoes, wedged
1 English cucumber (could use celery)
1 bag mesclun lettuce (or whatever kind of salad greens you like)
1 carrot, julienned
1 red sweet pepper
1 Spanish onion, finely sliced
½ pound chicken tenders (defrosted, if frozen)
1 tablespoon red curry paste
1 tablespoon white wine
1 tablespoon olive oil plus a little extra
1 tablespoon sour cream
12 fresh mint leaves-chopped

Brush naan bread with the extra olive oil, wrap in kitchen paper and microwave for one minute.

Boil rice with tumeric for color and flavor.

Combine in a bowl and gently toss, the mango, tomatoes, sliced cucumber, carrot, red pepper, onion, and greens of choice. Arrange tossed salad equally between the naan breads.

Combine the curry paste with the white wine and oil.

Heat marinade in a pan, add the chicken tenders, and cook through.

Combine the sour cream with the diced cucumber and mint to make the riata.

To serve: Create a large circle of rice on each of four plates and nestle the salad-filled naan breads in the center of each. Arrange chicken pieces on the top and dress with the riata.

If you wish, drizzle with zesty Italian salad dressing.

THE MAGIC OF THE SNOWSHOE HARE

Bunny rabbits also share our hideaway. Some of our rabbits wear a size 13 shoe. Their feet are as long as their body. It's truly amazing that they don't trip over them and can hop at all. During the summer months these rabbits are brown. This fall I thought I saw a new rabbit coming to visit. Each day he was looking different. From his feet, working upward, he was donning his camouflage coat of winter white. I was witness to one of Mother Nature's best magic tricks—the transformation of the snowshoe rabbit.

One lovely evening David and I were sitting on the front porch bench enjoying a glass of wine when an entire family of jackrabbits came hopping in. We watched Mommy, Daddy, and baby bunnies eat and play in the tall grass totally at ease and unaware of our presence as they hopped over and around each other. It was another chance to share the wonder of nature, to view and appreciate family life on another level.

I have an herb garden with a five-foot fence around it. The fence is to keep the deer and the rabbits out. I have watched the rabbits stretch and raise up as high as they could reach and then drop down to the ground to stretch out as far as they could stretch to try and figure a way over or under the fence to the growing salad bowl just out of reach. So far so good, the salad is all mine.

The same is not true for my Dad's garden. This year he put extra effort into building raised planting beds for his vegetables. He incorporated used brick, shake shingles, small logs, and strips of wood. Extensive netting was installed to keep the birds out of the blueberry patch. There is a five-foot-high fence around the perimeter.

Romaine lettuce has been on his list of vegetables for the garden since his move to the mountains. This year the time had come and one of the raised beds was planted with romaine seeds. He waited impatiently for the seeds to sprout and eagerly watched as the bright green leaves emerged from the ground, grew and formed beautiful heads of romaine lettuce. Every trip to the garden (which was at least twice a day), he would say, "Just look at that romaine!"

We were not allowed to cut and use it for salads. Oh, no, don't touch the lettuce. You can only look at it.

Unfortunately, the return of my snowshoe rabbits this season also meant the demise of the romaine, for the bunnies also had been watching it grow. My cute, furry, munchkin friends found a way into the garden and overnight had cut down, snacked on, played, and danced in the lettuce patch. Shredded pieces of leaves were all that was left of the prized heads of romaine.

Needless to say, the home grown salad bowl is empty this year. Despite best laid plans and sincere efforts, refills will only be obtained from the market. If you are lucky enough to beat the bunnies to the lettuce, here's what you do with it:

NORTH WOODS PEAR SALAD

This simple salad is a true taste sensation. The light, sweet-tart dressing is a perfect compliment to the pears, toasted walnuts, and feta cheese. YUMMY!

Serves 6

INGREDIENTS FOR THE DRESSING:

½ cup salad oil
3 tablespoons cider vinegar
¼ cup sugar
½ teaspoon celery seed
¼ teaspoon salt
Blend all ingredients and set aside.

INGREDIENTS FOR THE SALAD:

6 cups red leaf lettuce
1 pear, peeled and diced
*Pineapple juice
½ cup toasted walnuts or pecans
3 ounces crumbled feta or blue cheese

Lightly toast the nuts in a sauté pan over low heat, stirring constantly. Transfer to a plate to cool. Wash and spin dry the lettuce leaves. Place the lettuce on 6 salad plates, sprinkle with the pears, nuts and cheese. Drizzle the dressing over the top.

Note: If the pears need to be prepared ahead of time and held, place them in a bowl and cover them with pineapple juice to prevent discoloring.

Also be sure to purchase extra pears so that you can whip up the following recipe. It is the utmost delicious Pear Cake with Lemon Sauce.

PEAR CAKE WITH LEMON SAUCE

Serves 12

FOR THE CAKE:

2½ cups all-purpose flour
2 teaspoons baking powder
1 teaspoon salt
2 cups sugar
2/3 cups cooking oil
2 eggs, slightly beaten
1 teaspoon vanilla
3 cups finely chopped, peeled pears
½ cup chopped pecans

FOR THE SAUCE:

1 cup sugar
½ cup butter
½ cup buttermilk
1 tablespoon finely shredded lemon peel
1 tablespoon light corn syrup
1 teaspoon vanilla

For cake: grease a 13 x 9 inch baking pan; set aside. In a medium mixing bowl, combine flour, baking powder, and salt; set aside. In a large mixing bowl, combine the sugar, the cooking oil, eggs, vanilla. Add flour mixture and stir well. Stir in pears and pecans. (Batter will be stiff.) Spread batter into prepared pan. Bake in a 350 degree oven about 40 minutes or until a wooden toothpick inserted near the center comes out clean. Cool in pan on a wire rack while you make the sauce.

For sauce: in a medium saucepan, combine the 1 cup sugar, the butter, buttermilk, lemon peel and corn syrup. Cook and stir over medium heat until mixture boils; remove from heat. Stir in vanilla, cool slightly. Serve cake warm with the warm sauce.

YES, DEAR ...

What does the term "cat house" mean to you? Well, let me tell you about mine. It was a cold, October morning when I saw a small, skinny, black and orange calico cat. In our neck of the woods there are no stray cats. I was sure someone had merely dumped her off on the side of the road. Now that I had seen it, of course I had to help it.

I put food out for her, but the dog ate it. I just couldn't find a place to put food and water that Mattie couldn't get to. So I decided this poor kitty needed protection from the weather and a place for its food. Saturday morning when my husband asked me what was on his Honey-Do List, I said that I needed a cat house. "Are you nuts!" was the reply.

So that afternoon he built me a cat house with a shingled roof and insulated walls. It was perfect. I put a bowl of fresh water and another with cat food in the house and watched. Once again Mattie found the food first. She laid on her belly, stretched one long front leg into the cat house, carefully pulled the food bowl to her and ate it all.

Sunday morning when David asked what was on his Honey-Do List, I said we need to modify the cat house. "Are you nuts!" was the reply. That afternoon he remodeled the cat house. I was happy for awhile anyway—at least the cat could eat and drink.

The cat got bigger, bolder, and destructive. She began knocking over trash, catching my birds, and she ate all of the chipmunks. She had to go. So once again the live trap came out and we relocated kitty to a farm area with lots of mice and shelter. She came back. It took her a week, but she came back. So once again the live trap came out and this time kitty took a lot longer trip. She was successfully relocated this time. I do still have the cat house, and it is still empty.

Most cats eat birds, fish, and mice right? If our feral cat had showed an interest in these menu items, all would have been well. Unfortunately, she had a preference for chipmunk.

A local eagle would have served her up an elegant fare of fish drop dinner had she been around. Not often, but it does happen that an eagle that has been fishing the river will drop his prey en route to the dining room.

If you should have an eagle drop dinner by for you, here is what you might do with that fresh trout or salmon. We make fillet of salmon with a sweet pecan sauce. If I counted on the eagle to bring my fish, I would probably never have this wonderful meal. However, my white fish of choice is halibut or sea bass.

This is a fun meal to cook with a partner in the kitchen. So pour two glasses of wine and prepare to enjoy the evening and this great dinner with a friend.

FILLET OF SALMON

Serve with a fresh green salad topped with North Woods Dill-Dijon Vinaigrette (one of my bottled salad dressings.) A lemon tart for dessert would be the perfect finish.

Serves 4

1 cup pecan pieces
1 cup honey
¾ cup unsalted butter
¼ cup vegetable oil
4 salmon fillets, 4–6 ounces each
Salt and freshly ground black pepper

Preheat the oven to 350 degrees.

Spread the pecans in a single layer on a small baking sheet. Bake until aromatic and crisp, about 5 minutes, stirring 2-3 times to toast the pecans uniformly. Cool to room temperature.

To prepare the glaze, combine the honey, half the butter and the pecans in a small sauce pan. Over moderately high heat, cook until the pecans are coated in a glossy glaze, 7-10 minutes. Remove from the heat and keep warm.

In a large sauté pan, melt the remaining butter with the oil over high heat. Season the fish with salt and pepper to taste. Sauté until the fillets are firm to the touch, about 4 minutes per side. Transfer to serving plates and spoon with the glaze.

LEMON TART

Makes four 4½-inch tarts

INGREDIENTS FOR PASTRY:

- 1¼ cups all-purpose flour
- ¼ teaspoon salt
- 2 tablespoons sugar
- 3 tablespoons unsalted butter-chilled and cut into small pieces
- 2 tablespoons ice water
- ½ teaspoon freshly squeezed lemon juice

INGREDIENTS FOR THE FILLING:

- ½ cup freshly squeezed lemon juice
- ¼ cup sugar
- 3 eggs
- 3 egg yolks

INGREDIENTS FOR THE MERINGUE:

- 5 egg whites
- ¾ cup sugar

Preheat the oven to 425 degrees.

To make the pastry: Combine the flour, salt, and sugar in the work bowl of a food processor; pulse briefly to mix. Cut in the butter and the shortening with several quick pulses. Do not over mix. With the motor running, gradually pour in the ice water and the lemon juice and process just until the dough forms a mass around the blade. Turn the dough out onto a floured work surface and knead briefly. Gather the dough into a small ball, wrap in plastic, and refrigerate for at least 2 hours or up to 2 days.

To prepare the filling: Combine the lemon juice, sugar, eggs and egg yolks in a double boiler set over hot but not boiling water. Whisk to blend, then stir constantly with a wooden spoon until the mixture is the consistency of thick custard, about 12 minutes. Pour into a shallow dish and let cool completely, then cover with plastic wrap and refrigerate until firm, about 2 hours.

When ready to make the tarts, cut the dough into 4 equal pieces and roll each one into a circle 6-in. x $^{1}/_{8}$-in. thick. Line each of 4 tartlet molds 4½-inch-wide with a circle. Refrigerate the pastry for at least 20-30 minutes before baking. Cold pastry makes for a flakier crust. Prick the bottoms of lined pastry shells with a fork. Line the shells with foil and fill with dried beans (pastry weights) to prevent the dough from puffing up. Bake until the edges are browned and the dough is set, about 15 minutes. Remove the foil and beans and continue baking until the shell is uniformly brown, 3 to 5 minutes more. Be careful not to let the pastry scorch. Remove to a wire rack, unmold and cool completely.

To make the meringue:, beat the egg whites with the remaining ¾ cup sugar until the whites are stiff and shiny. Reduce the oven temperature to 350 degrees. Fill the shells with the lemon custard and place on a baking sheet. Divide the meringue among the four tart pans and use a knife to spread over the filling.

Bake until the meringue is lightly browned on top, about 15 minutes. Let cool slightly before serving.

HOW TO THROW ROCKS AT ELK

Elk do not belong in our little mountain hideaway. These massive, smelly, scraggly haired quadrupeds plow through everything. What they don't eat, they knock over. Occasionally they traverse our property as they migrate back up the mountain in the spring. As long as they don't linger and get destructive, I will allow them to trespass. This is how I used to think. Now I've learned to just stay out of the way.

The first time that I chased an elk was also the last time that I chased an elk. It was an early spring Sunday morning and David was sleeping in a bit. Being an early riser I was up, but not dressed, just going about the house in my pink flowered pajamas. As I start to get a little breakfast going, I see two cow elk saunter into the yard and start munching on some spilled bird seed that was around the base of the feeder. It didn't take long for them to finish what was on the ground and move on to the bird feeder itself. The feeder is nailed to a fence post. To better get at the feeder they attempted to knock down the post, fence and all, with head butts and by ramming it with their bodies. That was too much!

I ran outside still in my flowered pajamas, waving my arms and yelling at them. The elk did not care and did not move. So I picked up some small rocks and threw them. My throwing arm lacked the power to carry the rocks far enough. I had to get closer. Armed with more rocks I moved in and threw again. This time I hit my target. They moved back only a few feet, however, and looked down on me with bird seed speckled noses.

As they towered over me, I realized just how big they are (about 1000–1500 pounds to my 115 pounds). Slowly I backed up and returned to the house. The elk continued to attack my bird feeder and my fence. I decided to let them.

David had another approach when dealing with the elk. It was late on a Friday night and no moon was shining so it was totally black outside—until the motion light by the deer feeder came on. The animals that had come to feed that night were in the form of a small herd of elk. As I was watching them I heard the sound of a large dog barking on the front porch. Our dogs, Mattie and Cookie, had been kenneled up earlier in the evening so I was hearing a mystery dog. WOOF! WOOF! The dog on my front porch was tall (6'4"), hairy, wearing a blue plaid shirt and barking up a storm at the elk.

Despite his efforts to scare away our visitors with his ferocious bark, all they did was blink at him and continue to smash in the metal garbage cans that held the bird seed. I grabbed a saucepan and a lid, stepped outside clanging and banging and away they went through the brush.

Elk hunting is a popular sport in this neck of the woods. I'm not fond of this meat myself. But when I'm offered a package of elk steaks by a proud and successful hunter, I graciously accept the gift. Three years later when this same package has been in the freezer for this extended amount of time and the meat has freezer burn, I chop it up and cook it for the dog! Mattie will eat anything.

Many hunters do not clean up after themselves as well as they should, so Mattie helps with their housecleaning. She frequently brings home a partial elk leg or any other chunk of elk that has been left behind that she can get in her mouth and drag home.

Would you like to know how to make elk leg stew? Sure you would!

LEG OF ELK STEW — ALSO KNOWN AS — COUNTRY-STYLE SPLIT PEA SOUP

Partial leg of elk that the dog has dragged in during hunting season, hair, hoof, and all. Don't bother to pick the lice and ticks off, they float to the surface during cooking and can be easily skimmed off later.
Yield 14 cups.

My elk leg of choice is actually a ham bone—without the bugs.

2 quarts water
2 cups split green peas
1 large meaty ham bone
1 medium onion, chopped
1 medium potato, peeled and sliced
½ cup chopped celery
1 clove garlic, minced
½ teaspoon salt
¼ teaspoon pepper
1 bay leaf
2 carrots, peeled, and cut into small pieces
2 cups chicken broth or water (optional)*

Sort and wash peas; place in a Dutch oven. Cover with water 2 inches above peas; let soak overnight. Drain; add 2 quarts water and next 9 ingredients. Bring to a boil; cover, reduce heat, and simmer 3 hours, stirring occasionally.

Remove ham bone (or elk leg); cut off meat and dice and set aside. Discard bone and bay leaf. Transfer remaining mixture in batches to container of a food processor and process until smooth. Return mixture and meat to Dutch oven. Cover and simmer 5 minutes or until heated thoroughly.

Note: The soup can get quite thick, especially if it is refrigerated overnight. Stirring in 2 cups of chicken broth or water during reheating takes care of this problem.

YOU EAT — I EAT

One of the hardest facts of nature for me to accept is the food chain. Every living creature has to eat. This a fact of life. We feed the deer, the elk, the birds, the chipmunks, the squirrels, and anything else that cares to partake of the abundant supply of seeds, grains, apples, bread, and hay that we put out for them. We do this because we truly enjoy watching the animals come in to visit us on a regular basis. However, some of the consequential viewings are not so good.

On one particular Sunday morning, I had come inside after filling the bird feeders and throwing a little extra seed on the ground for the birds that like to dig and scratch. My first cup of coffee was steaming in my hands as the birds were flying in for their breakfast. While I watched this peaceful scene, a sharp-shinned hawk swooped in and carried away one of my little birds. The screaming still echoes in my mind.

That hawk lived in our trees lurking around for a long time. One of his favorite perches was a post on the deck at the back of the cabin. He was a strikingly beautiful bird and I knew he had to eat too. I did wish, however, that he would change his location for take-out to Arby's or McDonald's. My neighbor had a great horned owl carry off a chicken once. Thankfully, I did not witness that.

I like dogs and have two of my own. Cookie is a 15-year-old Malamute-Doberman mix. Mattie is a 4-year-old Black Labrador retriever. I like wolves too. I think they are magnificent, but wild and frightening.

It was a cold, November Saturday morning. David was away at Apple Cup—the annual Washington State and University of Washington football rivalry game. It is a "guys" weekend that a group of about 15 look forward to every year. My point being that I was all alone with the beast that had entered the yard. It looked like a dog only rougher. The teeth were huge and jagged when he smiled at me. He had pointed ears and a long bushy tail. The coloring of his fur resembled scruffy tree bark. He advanced into the open, came toward the house and stopped. As he looked from side to side, I could see a blood chilling look in his menacing eyes. I just stood there staring with my mouth hanging open. I knew that I recognized him from the story of the *Three Little Pigs* and I was just waiting for him to blow my house in.

Never had I been so close to something like this. My dogs were in the kennel and must have sensed the presence of my intruder because they started a commotion that should have raised the dead. Instantly my visitor was gone. Coyotes share these woods with us as do wolves. My best guess is that my early morning visitor was a wolf. I have seen many a coyote cross the road in front of me when I'm driving these mountain roads. This animal was larger, darker and drooling. Because of the lasting impression of fear this sighting left me with I purchased a pistol, a snub-nose 38 revolver to be precise, and learned to shoot. I am now Mountain Woman—a pistol packing mama.

Sadly, we lost our Cookie dog. She was struck by a car and killed the Spring of 2008. Her final resting place is in her favorite warm, sunny spot out by the deer feeder. I have planted it with roseglow barberry, golden euonymus and a small pile of rocks. None of which the dear will eat.

Mattie is now a house dog. It brings tears to my eyes to see her still sit and watch and wait everyday for her best friend to come home.

CHIPMUNK'S COFFEE BREAK?

"Shopping, let's go to town shopping," said the chipmunk to the Cadillac. So determined was he, that on Monday morning he hitched a ride to town. He found a comfortable place to ride somewhere under the hood or on the undercarriage of the car and settled in for the 40-minute trip to town. When we arrived at David's auto repair shop, he parked the car in the usual place.

As we were walking across the parking lot to the office, Mr. Chips (the chipmunk) ran ahead as if to lead the way. Until that point, we had been totally unaware of our passenger. We looked at each other and shook our heads wondering what the poor little guy would do in the big city of Selah. His little tail going around the corner of the building was the last we saw of him until about 10:00 that morning.

Coffee break time brought excitement to the Pelzels. Dottie, our secretary, was up on a chair screaming and on her way to the desk top. She'd seen a mouse and it was a huge mouse, maybe even a giant rat. Customers in the office were heading for chairs or out the door. Wait, there it is! Mr. Chips was back and he had to go. He dashed through the open bathroom door and jumped into the toilet.

Oops!

While David was fishing him out of the water, I found a box. We dried him with a shop towel, put some paper in the box for him to nest in and hoped that he would be comfortable until it was time to go home. The rest of the day was uneventful. Upon returning home, we opened the box and released Mr. Chips. As we watched him scurry away apparently unharmed, we hoped that one trip to town was enough for him. Chipmunks are not supposed to bathe in the toilet. We have had other chipmunks take the ride to town, but Mr. Chips is the only one we have been able to return to the wild.

Mergansers, Harlequins, and Mallards are among a few of the

ducks we see on the river. Geese are frequently enjoying the water there also. Sometimes all you can see of the ducks are their little duck butts, a few feathers and flapping feet as they feed upside down in the water. The fluffy, baby ducklings are so cute as they float and bob around in the water. Occasionally we are lucky enough to see a hen paddle by with her fuzzy brood all piled on her back.

For the first time ever I saw beavers in the wild. Just watching them swim in the river was amazing for me. Nature's small lumberjacks are dedicated to their work. These little guys are very busy hauling branches and twigs down river to their dams. The bark chewed from trees and other signs of cutting and harvesting of small trees and shrubs is undeniable evidence of their construction work. They are cute little animals but very destructive.

Our river is also home to fish such as trout and salmon. Fishing is not my thing as not only are they stinky and slimy, they also give me a rash (allergies). Don't forget that snakes and spiders share the waters as well. They hide, slither and crawl among the moss covered rocks just laying in wait for your bare toes.

There is nothing quite like a good book, a lawn chair, and splashing your feet in the refreshing water of the river on a hot summer day—as long as you don't get that lurking snake between your toes and spiders crawling up your legs. Who am I trying to kid? I keep my tennis shoes on when I get in the water, which isn't often.

One summer we were catching up on a little yard work and discovered a family of baby mice living in a small nest between the potting bench and the animal feed cans. We left the tiny, pink, sightless creatures alone. I don't want mice in the house, but outside I won't bother them. The next day we checked on the babies only to find a snake in the nest and the mice gone. Wonder what happened?

Mice for dinner are not listed on my menu. That is how I differ from the snake. My preference for tiny, pink creatures is shrimp. You must try this.

FETTUCCINE ALREDO WITH SHRIMP, ASPARAGUS, AND MUSHROOMS

Serves 12

1 pound fettuccine
2 pounds fresh asparagus, cut into 1-inch pieces
1 tablespoon unsalted butter
8 ounces white mushrooms, sliced
2 cups heavy cream
2 cups half-and-half
1 cup fresh lemon juice
2 cups grated Parmigiano Reggiano cheese
½ teaspoon salt
Coarsely ground black pepper to taste
Nutmeg to taste
¾ to 1 pound shrimp, cooked and peeled and deveined.

Cook fettuccine according to package directions, adding asparagus during the last 2 minutes. Drain well.

Melt butter in a large skillet. Add mushrooms and cook until tender, 2-3 minutes.

Combine cream, half-and-half and lemon juice in a large deep skillet; cook over medium heat about 3 minutes. Add pasta mixture to cream mixture; stir well. Add cheese, nutmeg, salt and pepper and cook, tossing fettuccine, until sauce thickens slightly, about 1 minute. Add shrimp and mushrooms. Serve warm. Serves 12.

DAVID'S STORY (IN HIS OWN WORDS)

I graduated from Selah High School in 1970. Upon graduation, I didn't know what I was going to do or become. I had only been a "C" student. My Dad had been a mechanic his whole life and during my growing up years I had helped him with repair work on cars, trucks and tractors. So I thought that becoming a mechanic would be a good choice.

That summer, after graduation, I went to Yakima Valley College to register for the automotive course they offered. When I sat down with the sign-up instructor, he said that the class was full. When I gave him my name, he asked if my dad's name was Connie. I said that it was. He then told me that he had worked with my dad back in the 50's for a company by the name of Bell Wyman's Auto Repair. He also said that he would definitely make room for me in the class.

During two years at YVC, I worked part-time for my Dad's auto repair business and upon graduation from YVC began working there full-time.

Soon after, Dad was diagnosed with stomach cancer. His treatments made him too ill to work and he offered me the business. Of course I was scared but knew it was the right thing to do.

I didn't have but $100 cash to start with. Thank goodness I had all of his equipment and tools to use. At 20 years of age, I also didn't have any established line of credit. The first thing I had to do was make contact with all of the people that Dad had done business with over the years and ask for credit. They all agreed as long as I paid everything off on a monthly basis. This shouldn't be a problem, I thought, as Dad had a good client base and they all knew me. I had been repairing their vehicles for two years already.

The first week came to an end and I'd had more than enough work to pay for the parts and still make a profit. However, my first bank deposit set me back a bit. A customer from Oregon had written me a bad check for $400. Remember, I only had $100 to start, and I was in shock.

I thought to myself, is this what it is going to be like dealing with the public?

It took a few months, but I did catch up with the person who wrote the check and he made good on it. Thank God for that!

Month by month I was getting busier and busier. Another mechanic was needed and within three years a larger building was needed as well as more mechanics. I have been in this second location for 27 years, have five technicians and a secretary. Things are going well.

Mary's Note

My man works hard and deserves special treats.
The following recipe is one of his favorites.
It is a jazzed up version of fried chicken.

CRISPY CHICKEN MEDALLIONS WITH MUSTARD SAUCE

Serves 6

6 boneless, skinless chicken breasts
Salt and freshly ground black pepper
2 cups panko (Japanese-style breadcrumbs)
1 tablespoon chopped fresh lemon thyme
1 cup all-purpose flour
4 large eggs, beaten
2 tablespoons extra virgin olive oil
2 cloves of garlic, chopped
1 shallot, chopped
1 cup dry sherry
1 cup heavy whipping cream
¾ cup sour cream
Heaping teaspoon Dijon mustard
1 heaping teaspoon herb mustard, such as herbes de Provence
2 teaspoons whole-grain mustard

Preheat oven to 350 degrees.

Place the chicken breasts on a board and cover with plastic wrap. Using a meat mallet, pound the chicken breasts to even them out and flatten them until they are about ½-inch thick. Season well with salt and pepper.

To bread the chicken, combine the panko and lemon thyme in a food processor, and process until the panko is crushed and the mixture is well blended; transfer to a pie plate. Place the flour on a plate and the eggs in a pie plate. Dredge the chicken breasts in the flour, dip them in the egg, then coat well with the panko mixture.

Heat the olive oil in a large sauté pan over medium heat until hot. Add as many chicken breasts as will fit in the pan, without over crowding and fry until golden brown, about 2 minutes per side. Transfer to a sheet pan, and continue with the remaining chicken breasts.

Place the sheet pan in the oven and bake the chicken just until the breasts are cooked through, about 5 minutes. Transfer to a plate and keep warm.

Meanwhile, to prepare the sauce, remove and discard the panko crumbs from the oil in the sauté pan. Set the pan over high heat and heat until hot. Add the garlic, shallots, and sherry, reduce heat and simmer until about ¼ cup of liquid remains, about 5 minutes. Add the sour cream and mustards, and mix well. Season with salt and pepper to taste.

To serve, place the chicken on a serving platter and drizzle with some of the sauce. Serve hot with remaining sauce on the side.

GRACIE'S STORY

Once upon a time, in the city of Selah, Washington, a city employee, Vern Ford, was about his daily duties of reading water meters. This day turned out to be a very special day to many because of his alertness.

As Mr. Ford was reading a particular meter, out of the corner of his eye he saw something move. Upon investigation, he discovered a very tiny baby kitten. He went into the closest establishment, which was our car repair shop. He entered my office and said "Hey, MJ, there is a kitten under the oil barrel in back of the shop." My response was, "No, there's not." If there was a kitten out there, then I would have to do something about it and I didn't have time to deal with a kitten. I went out to have a look anyway.

To my dismay, there was indeed a kitten under the barrel. This tiny creature was no bigger than my fist, covered with oil and grease, blind, and could barely stand. Scared to death, the poor thing was slowly turning circles. Apparently it had been abandoned by the mother because it couldn't keep up.

I wrapped the kitten in a shop towel and took it to the vet. Can this kitten be saved or should we help it to go away? What do we do? If Mr. Ford had been reading water meters just one day later, he would have found a dead kitten. That night the temperatures dropped to below freezing and she would not have survived. She was blind because of conjunctivitis. This we could treat with medication. She was very weak and wobbly, partly because she was so young, but mainly because of the fleas. She was about four weeks old and horribly flea infested. Upon further investigation, we discovered that baby kitty was a girl.

I named her Gracie that day for I felt that by the grace of God she had been found and I was determined to save her. This was easier said than done because I already had another cat at home—Corky. Gracie had to be kept in quarantine in the bathroom because of the fleas and the eye infection. The eyes healed up in a few days, however the flea problem took two months. Gracie was too young for flea treatments so David and I had to bathe her daily and pick off the fleas with tweezers. We took off close to 100 fleas. They were literally sucking the life out of her.

At first, we could contain her in a box. As she grew and got stronger, we moved her to the bathtub. Finally, she had the run of the bathroom. Dancing around a kitten and watching for fleas —not fun! We also had to teach our baby to eat and drink. Saving Gracie had turned into a 24-hour-a-day job.

I think that it is because of her many baths that Gracie is a water baby today. She loves to shower, take a bath, play in the sink, and drink from the faucets in the sink and the tub. She does a thing that I call "paw drinking". When water is running into the bathtub, she will sit on the side of the tub and swipe at the stream of water with her paws. She then drinks from her paws. The wetter she gets, the better she likes it. I can't keep my floors clean. They always have Gracie's wet foot prints all over them.

To Gracie, I am Mommy. She is a sweet little soul and has a very loving personality. Wake-up time at our house is 4:30 a.m. Gracie has her alarm set also. She purrs so loudly that she whistles. (Drooling goes along with the purring also.) The sideways chortle run is most entertaining. This is when she arches her back and carries her long, fluffy tail high in the air. She runs sideways, prancing, strutting and chortling—just coaxing you to come and play with her. It's like watching a bubble of happiness float around.

Who could ask for a better sales associate. She helps me sell cookbooks, bread mixes, and baskets. When Gracie is in town with me, she loves to ride in the grocery cart with her front feet draped over the front edge of the cart. She likes to go fast. As long as the cart is moving, everything is just fine. If I stop to look at an item on the shelf, so does she. Her white fluffy paws are constantly swatting at anything within reach. Craft Warehouse knows her as the kitty that cooks. They let her play with the ribbons while I shop. Dunbar Jewelers is her favorite stop. She loves the sparkling jewelry. Best of all, she is my companion and friend and I don't know what I would do without her.

She has developed into a beautiful animal. Her body is mostly black. She has little white cheeks, a white streak between her eyes, and her chest and tummy are white. She is a very long cat with four white fluffy paws. Her hair varies in length from one to two inches except for her back legs. As she walks away from you, it looks like she is wearing pantaloons because of the four inches of fluffy fur that encompass the length of her legs. How that girl can strut her stuff!

She and I have one thing in common—a love of expensive seafood. Her little nose never quits wiggling as she sniffs the aromas of crab, lobster, and shrimp while in the seafood department of the grocery store. I take her there just to tease her. However, when I make the following crab casserole at home, she always gets her share!

NORTH WOODS CRAB CASSEROLE

Serves 4 People and 1 Cat

1 pound fresh lump crab meat or two 6 1/2-ounce cans
2 eggs
1 cup milk
1 tablespoon Worcestershire sauce
½ cup melted butter
¼ teaspoon salt
½ teaspoon white ground pepper, or to your taste
1 cup Parmesan bread crumbs—reserve some extra for sprinkling on top

Beat eggs, add milk, Worcestershire sauce, butter, bread crumbs, salt and pepper. Add crab meat. Pour into greased casserole and sprinkle with reserved bread crumbs. Bake at 350 degrees 30-40 minutes, until nicely browned.

Variation: Slice up 6 button mushrooms (white or cremini), add ½ cup chopped sweet onion and sauté together in a small amount of olive oil. Stir this into the crab mixture and then pour into the greased casserole. After removing the finished casserole from the oven, sprinkle with fresh chopped parsley and fresh chopped tomatoes.

GRACIE AND THE SPIDER NIGHTMARE

One restless night sleep eluded me. It was one of those toss and turn nights and finally I drifted off to a light wake-sleep phase. My tossing and turning was interrupted by the sight of a huge black and white spider on the stairs. As this hairy eight-legged arachnid ascended the stairs, I screamed. Now aware of my presence, it turned and methodically advanced toward me, one leg at a time. Its beady eyes never left mine. The only weapon at my disposal was a grungy tennis shoe. All of a sudden, the spider raised up and leaped for me. I hurled the shoe. Bulls eye! Down it went. The spider hit the floor with a thud. Lying there on the floor wiggling, it slowly turned into my black and white kitten, Gracie. I had cold-cocked my cat! With tears running down my face, I awoke to find Gracie curled up in bed beside me washing her face with her big, fluffy, white paws.

My dreams can always be explained by daily events. Gracie is associated with spiders because she eats them. Many is the time I have interrupted her in the middle of a meal with a spider leg hanging out of her mouth.

That morning when I looked in the mirror, there it was—another spider bite. It's no wonder I have dreams about them. They share my bed. Certain times of the year are worse than others. Unfortunately, they do consider me a delicacy. My white Scandinavian skin frequently sports red bumps and itchy blotches from nightly spider feeding frenzies. Mountain Woman that I now am, I have discovered an innovative way to use these annoying, obnoxious, and sometimes frightening creatures to the max. This treat is especially fun at Halloween time.

FRESH FUZZY SPIDER CUPCAKES

Wash and line dry 12 black fuzzy spiders. Note: for fluffier fuzzy spiders, dry in the drier on gentle cycle for one minute.

**If you prefer, use one black or orange jellybean for the spider body and small pieces of black string licorice for the eight legs. Be sure to give each faux spider personality by adding tiny pieces of licorice for eyes.*

Makes a dozen cupcakes.

12 black and orange jellybeans and black string licorice*
  or black fuzzy spiders
1 box of cake mix—your flavor choice
1 can of white fluffy frosting

Bake cupcakes following directions on a box mix of choice and frost with white frosting from a can. Be sure to use white frosting so that your decorations will show up. Top each cake with one fuzzy spider.

MY FRIEND, THE JUNKIE

Peanut is a Douglas squirrel—very cute, brown in color with an orangish-tan tummy, tiny ears, sparkling little eyes, and a big bushy tail. She is a sunflower seed junkie.

Alongside my gift shop stands a brown, Rubbermaid® garbage can. This can is used to store wild bird seed. Each morning as part of my daily routine, all of the bird feeders are cleaned and filled with fresh seeds. One morning I noticed a small hole in the lid of my feed can about the size of a nickel. Each day the hole became increasingly bigger until it had approximately a four inch diameter. Obviously something with sharp teeth wanted at the bird seed. So far, I had not seen the creator of the hole.

Approaching the gift shop (and the feed can) with my arms full of paperwork and other necessary items for the day, I heard a loud scratching noise. I stopped and listened, unsure as to where it was coming from. Then a little brown head popped up through the hole in the lid. With a little more scratching and wiggling, out popped Peanut. She scampered across the yard and up the nearest fir tree. From atop a high branch she chattered and chirped her annoyance at me for disturbing her breakfast.

Peanut has continued to enlarge on the "entrance" to the can and has pretty much taken up permanent residence there. I have learned to knock on the side of the can and say "Peanut are you home?" prior to lifting the lid to obtain bird seed for the birds. When the level of the seed drops too low, Peanut can't jump out and I have been surprised with a scrambling squirrel in my face. We have become friends and Peanut has become social with my customers. She will walk the handrails and strut her stuff or sit on the can lid and chirp at them. She has become a favorite attraction.

When we installed underground sprinklers, we had to move Peanut's can to the other side of the gift shop. This created a very entertaining afternoon as we watched her look for the can. She raced up, down, around, and back and forth on the handrails of the porch. She ran up the steps and down the steps. She was all over the prior location of her home. She would raise up on her haunches and chirp at us. She was truly annoyed. By the next morning she was once again in the can. Ah—home, sweet home!

You might think that squirrels only eat seeds and nuts—nope. Peanut likes cookies too. The following are her favorites:

NORTH WOODS APRICOT BARS

Makes 32 bars

2/3 cups dried apricots
½ cup soft butter
½ cup granulated sugar
1 cup sifted flour
½ teaspoon baking powder
¼ teaspoon salt
½ cup whole-bran cereal
1 cup brown sugar
½ teaspoon vanilla
2 eggs-well beaten
½ cup walnuts
Confectioner's sugar

Cover apricots with water* bring to a boil and simmer 10 minutes.

Drain , cool and chop.

Blend butter, sugar and ½ cup flour until crumbly. Stir in cereal. Pat into bottom of ungreased jelly roll pan. Bake at 350 degrees for 25 minutes.

Sift together remaining ½ cup flour, salt and baking powder. Set aside. Beat eggs then add brown sugar. Mix into dry ingredients. Add vanilla, nuts and apricots. Mix and spread over baked layer. Bake at 350 degrees for 30 minutes. Sprinkle with confectioner's sugar when cool.

**Feel free to substitute brandy for the water or perhaps a little orange or cherry liqueur.*

NORTH WOODS CHRISTMAS

A little snow or more—wow, isn't it beautiful! Winter holds its own challenges. Snow removal is your job. The county has big equipment for clearing the passes and the main highway only. We live across a bridge and down a dirt/gravel lane, around a corner, and then down a smaller wooded lane/trail to the house. If we don't shovel and dig out, we don't get out. Of course since all of the shovel handles had been whittled into roasting sticks over the summer, another trip to the hardware store is in order.

Two or three inches of new snow is no big deal. Two or three feet, now that's a big deal. One particularly bad winter season there was an accumulation of 14 feet over night. Our snow removal equipment consists of two snow throwers, a tractor, and an assortment of shovels. No matter how hard we tried to hide the shovels, most of them have broken handles. Dad could not rest until he felt there were enough roasting sticks for friends and family.

One evening we came home to two feet of fresh, white, gloriously, fluffy snow. I couldn't resist, was out of the truck, out of my clothes and off for a roll. It was cold, very cold and very fun. It was even more fun when David joined me. The hot tub followed, then a second roll in the snow. We were like a couple of little kids squealing with each cold flake. Crazy? Yup, sometimes we are. That's why we live here.

Because of our location, we get to do some activities that most people don't at Christmas time. David has started putting Christmas lights on the bridge. No one had ever done that here before. All the local residents enjoy the lights, and I have found that I count on them at night so that I don't drive by my own bridge in the dark. There have been nights that I had to turn around and come back.

Our Christmas tree is always in the great room. This is a large room that was included with the remodel of the cabin during our second year of ownership. It is a comfortable and inviting room with vaulted ceilings, tile floor, knotty pine walls, and a propane heat stove with natural looking logs for a 'real fire" look without the mess. The corner walls that border the stove are made from rocks that David and I hand selected and hauled from the river ourselves. (I don't think that you are supposed to do that.)

Let's get back to the Christmas tree. It is usually about 20 feet tall. Bringing this towering evergreen into the house is an event of its own. There is only one way in and one way out. We obtain a tree cutting permit and go in search of the perfect tree. That is the easy part. Once at home the tree has to be wrapped tightly in a tarp with ropes. The sides of the front door frame are wrapped with blankets for protection. The tree is then shoved up to the door opening with the base at the door and the tip pointing outward. Now the fun really begins. One person on either side of the door holds the blankets up. Two people from inside the house brace themselves to pull the tree inside. Two people push from the outside, trying for leverage. Sometimes this process goes smoothly, but not often. About four years ago was the funniest entrance of all, but someone could have been hurt. Ronnie and David were pushing from the outside. My Dad said he could handle the base from the inside. Push, shove, grunt, 1-2-3-, push, shove grunt, 1-2-3 oooooh oooooh, OH OH!! With a mighty shove from outside, the huge tree surged into the house. Yeah! It's in! But where is Dad? He is flat out on his back on the floor under the tree. He was bruised a bit, his back was sore and he had fir needles sticking out of his nose, but basically okay.

Decorating a tree of this size is not a simple task. Definitely not my job. I'm only 5'4". The use of an orchard ladder is the only way. This is very unsteady on tile floors. I remember hearing a large crash and rushing from the family room to the great room and finding David in the tree instead of on the ladder—not good. Our daughter Danielle's approach was to get a long stick with a nail on the end and using this tool to apply tinsel. She reminds me of her Grandpa with the shovel handles. Danielle is grown now. I've taught her how to hold her wine glass in one hand and the tinsel stick in the other. She is an assistant professor of ophthalmology with a PhD in vision science at U.T. Southwestern in Dallas, Texas. She's married to a lovely man, Peter. Baby Peyton Robert arrived in 2009 just after Thanksgiving.

Ronnie has taken over the job of putting the lights on the tree. He does a great balancing act on the ladder and sometimes uses Danielle's stick to aid in hanging the lights. So far he has not crashed into the tree.

Ron and Danielle have had an on-going contest to see who can have the most letters after their names. Currently Ron is ahead. He is an E.A., F.C.A., M.A.A., M.B.A. (Enrolled Actuary, Fellow in the Conference of Consulting Actuaries, Member in American Academy of Actuaries, Masters in Business Administration). However, Danielle has just passed an exam in England that has made her a Fellow in the British Society of Vision Science. There are only 92 members world-wide. This means that she has more letters coming. I can't keep up. Yes, we are very proud of our children!

At Christmas time everyone expects cookies. Ronnie's favorite has always been the chocolate/vanilla pinwheel and Danielle's is the candy cane. David and I really enjoy my specialty—the brandy infused fruitcake! Yeah, yeah, I know fruitcake has a bad reputation. Everybody hates it—so fine—I won't share that recipe with you. However, here are the cookie recipes. These cookies are a family Christmas tradition (so is the fruitcake).

CHRISTMAS CHOCOLATE/VANILLA PINWHEEL COOKIES

Makes about 4 dozen

1¼ cups butter softened
1½ cups confectioner's sugar
1 egg
3 cups all-purpose flour
¼ teaspoon salt
¼ cup Italian cocoa
½ cup finely chopped chocolate chips or the mini kind
1 teaspoon vanilla

Mix thoroughly butter, sugar and egg. Blend in flour and salt. Divide dough in half. Stir ¼ cup cocoa and chocolate chips into one half. Form each half of the dough into a ball. Wrap individually in plastic wrap and chill for 1 hour. On a lightly floured surface, roll vanilla dough into a rectangle, 16 x 9 inches. Roll the chocolate dough to the same size. Place the chocolate layer on top of the vanilla layer. Roll the chocolate and vanilla layered dough to 3/16-inch thick. Roll up tightly. Wrap and chill at least 8 hours.

Heat oven to 400 degrees. Cut rolls into ¼ inch slices. If dough crumbles while cutting, let warm slightly. Place 1 inch apart on an ungreased cookie sheet. Bake about 8 minutes. Immediately remove from baking sheet. Cool. You do not want the cookies to brown on the edges.

CHRISTMAS CANDY CANE COOKIES

It's just not Christmas without these cookies.

Makes about 4 dozen

½ cup butter, softened
½ cup shortening
1 cup confectioner's sugar
1 egg
1½ teaspoons almond extract
1 teaspoon vanilla
2½ cups all-purpose flour
1 teaspoon salt
½ teaspoon red food color
½ cup crushed peppermint candy
½ cup granulated sugar

Heat oven to 375 degrees. Mix thoroughly butter, shortening, confectioner's sugar, egg and flavorings. Blend in flour and salt. Divide dough in half; blend food coloring into one half.

Shape 1 teaspoon dough from each half into a 4-inch rope. For smooth, even ropes, roll them back and forth on lightly floured board. Place ropes side by side; press together lightly and twist. Complete the cookies one at a time. Place on ungreased baking sheet. Curve top down to form handle of cane.

Bake about 9 minutes or until set and only very, very lightly browned. Mix candy and granulated sugar. Immediately sprinkle cookies with candy mixture; remove from baking sheet. Cookies must be sprinkled while hot or the candy/sugar mixture will not stick.

THE NORTH WOODS CHRISTMAS FRUITCAKE

OK, as long as you insist, here is the fruitcake recipe. Keep in mind that this is a family secret. You must promise not to share it with anyone.

Makes 2 large loaf cakes

INGREDIENTS FOR CAKE:

- 1 cup white sugar
- 3 teaspoons cinnamon
- 1 teaspoon cloves
- 1⅔ cups hot applesauce
- 2 teaspoon baking soda
- ½ cup shortening
- 2½ cups flour
- 1 cup walnut halves (and extra for garnish)
- 1 cup whole Brazil nuts (Leave these whole. They make pretty white circles when you cut into the cake.)
- 1 (8-ounce) package whole dates
- 1 (16-ounce) container red candied cherries—save some out for garnish
- 1 (8-ounce) container green candied cherries—save some out for garnish
- 1 (8-ounce) container candied mixed fruit
- 1 (8-ounce) container candied pineapple

FOR GLAZE:

- 1 cup white sugar
- ½ cup rum or orange juice or Triple Sec liquor
- ½ cup water

Heat applesauce in a sauce pan, then stir in soda and shortening to melt.

Put fruits and nuts into a large bowl (remember to set some aside for garnish). Sprinkle with 1 cup of sugar and toss to coat. Combine cinnamon, cloves, and flour. Stir in applesauce mixture. Stir in nuts and fruits. Lightly grease 2 pans with shortening and then line with parchment paper. After the paper has been fitted to the pan, lightly grease it with shortening. Pour batter into 2 large loaf pans. Garnish the top of the cakes with the reserved walnut halves and the cherries. I cut the cherries in half so they lay nicely on top of the cake.

Bake at 350 degrees for about 1½ hours. Remove from oven and let sit in pans for about 10 minutes. Remove from pans, place on wire racks and cool slightly while you make the glaze.

To make the glaze:

Mix water and sugar. Bring to a boil and stir until sugar dissolves. Stir in the rum, orange juice, or liquor.

Place the cakes in a large sheet cake pan with a 1-inch rim. Slowly spoon the glaze over the cake, over the sides and on both ends. Raise the cakes lightly so that the glaze flows underneath the cake and soaks up the glaze from the bottom as well. Keep spooning the glaze on until it all has been absorbed by the cakes. Be patient. This takes a little time, but it is worth the effort.

Allow the cake to cool then wrap in plastic wrap and then in foil. Allow to sit for a couple of days, then eat it or freeze it. It is really good while still warm also but may fall apart when cutting. It will freeze and keep beautifully until the holidays. When taking cake from the freezer, unwrap while still in the frozen state. The cake is deliciously sticky and the paper comes off easier when the cake is still frozen. Serve on your best plate.

IT'S SNOWING—AGAIN!

Along with the snow comes the hungry animals. Sometimes for a really close look, Ron will drizzle a trail of feed from the feeder to the side windows of the house and then make little piles of feed. The deer come right up to the window and stare at us while they eat. How special is that! Sometimes the deer are grumpy and put on a really good show sparring for the biggest pile of seed.

After a particularly heavy snow, I was headed to town for groceries and errands. Oh my gosh, what was that! I could see something little and black jumping in a snow bank. It sunk into the soft snow, ran across the road and jumped in the snow bank left by the snow plow and sunk again. Again (I could now tell that it was a kitten) the animal ran across the road and into the snow bank on the other side. It was frantic, scared, and could not clear the snow. There was no way that I could catch it. Even though the Cat House was currently empty and had room for a border. Continuing my trip to town, I felt bad knowing that the kitten surely wouldn't survive the day.

Three weeks later and another town day, I was on my way home. There she was. Same kitty and same location. She had made it through. Hooray!

On October 31st we were at the Lodge for dinner and a Halloween Party. The entertainer for the evening announced, "Look outside. It is snowing." The whole room cheered, including stupid me. It is now May 1st and we still have snow on the ground. One of us is not cheering now—grumble, growl, shovel. Enough already!

We get really tired of the winter snows and chills. But this soup is a favorite to help keep those chills away. We look forward to its winter warmth.

BUTTERNUT SQUASH AND ITALIAN SAUSAGE SOUP

Serves 4-6

1 large butternut squash, about 3 pounds, halved and seeded
2 tablespoons vegetable oil
½ teaspoon salt
Freshly ground pepper
½ pound sweet Italian sausage, removed from casings
1 large onion, chopped
6 cloves garlic, minced
1 tablespoon chopped fresh sage, plus 12 whole leaves
1 teaspoon chopped fresh marjoram
6 cups light chicken stock or broth
1 teaspoon cider vinegar or lemon juice
½ cup heavy cream
2 tablespoons butter

Preheat the oven to 400 degrees.

Lightly coat the squash halves with 1 teaspoon vegetable oil. Season the inside with salt and pepper and place cut-side down on a baking sheet lined with parchment paper. Bake until very tender, about 45 minutes. When the squash is cool enough to handle, scoop out the flesh and reserve. Discard the peel.

In a large saucepan over medium-high heat, add the remaining vegetable oil and, when hot but not smoking, add the sausage. Cook until golden brown, about 4 minutes. Add the onions and cook, stirring, until the onions wilt and are starting to caramelize, about 6 minutes. Add the garlic, sage and marjoram, and cook, stirring, for 1 minute. Add the cooked squash and chicken stock, stir well to combine, and bring to a boil. Reduce the heat to low, and simmer for 30 minutes stirring occasionally.

In batches in a food processor, puree soup. Strain into a large sauce pan. Add the cider vinegar and stir to combine. Add the cream and adjust seasonings to taste.

In a small sauté pan, cook the butter over medium-high heat until it begins to turn brown around the edges. Add the whole sage leaves and cook until crisp, 1-2 minutes. Transfer the leaves to paper towels and drain.

Serve the soup in bowls, garnished with the crispy sage leaves.

FUNNY MOUNTAIN MAN

Keep in mind that not all hazards in the north woods are caused by the little creatures of the woodlands or by the actions of Mother Nature. If I am Mountain Woman, then my husband is Mountain Man. The following is the story of how a Mountain Man fixes a water leak. Once upon a time there was a drip, just a little drip of water.

One of life's most annoying inconveniences is when a household appliance, a piece of electrical equipment, or a tool that you rely on fails to do its required task. In this particular case, the washing machine is the object of my frustration.

It was laundry day. While sorting the dirty clothes in preparation for washing, I noticed a small amount of water on the bathroom floor in front of the washing machine. Assuming that it was residual water from the morning shower splashes and drips, I wiped it up with a towel and didn't think any more about it.

The next day, there was more water in the same place. This was not good. I did not have time to deal with a leaking washing machine. Once again I wiped up the water hoping that somehow a miracle would happen and there would not be more. By evening, all was still dry so I went to bed that night no longer concerned about a leak.

The next morning, I went into the bathroom to find my kitty, Gracie, playing and splashing in the puddle of water that had flowed from under the machine. Obviously this water leak was not going to fix itself.

Mountain Man David investigated the problem. After removing the front lower portion of the machine, he found a small, steady drip. To correct the problem he rolled up a towel and placed it in the area of the drip. We left the front of the machine open, and for two weeks, I continued to exchange wet towels for dry towels.

Super Bowl Sunday was coming up and we had invited a houseful of guests over to watch the big game on TV. Neither one of us wanted to have a disassembled washer and a wet floor mess in the bathroom. So David proceeded to put the lower panel back on the machine and clean up the mess. To this end I hear, "Hey Honey, where are the screws?"

"What screws?" I replied.

"I need the screws that I laid on the bathroom counter two weeks ago."

Well, for all I knew the cat had buried them in the litter box. After two weeks, there was no telling where the screws had gone to. David used some that he scrounged from who knows where that weren't "quite right". It didn't matter to me what screws he used. I was just happy that the machine was back together and that the floor was dry!

We had a great afternoon with friends. Everyone brought snacks and beverages. The sodas, beer, and wine were kept well chilled by shoving them in the three-foot-deep snow bank on the deck. Some white-tailed deer even wandered in to feed at the deer feeder, which delighted our city slicker friends.

The next day I asked David how he had stopped the leak in the washing machine. His reply was "I don't know. It just stopped leaking. I guess it fixed itself."

This made no sense to me. It was impossible unless there was a built in self repair cycle. However, there was no water on the floor. David went on to work and I prepared to do laundry.

As I loaded the machine with dirty clothes, I still wondered how it had healed itself. The soap was poured in and the clothes were loaded so I slammed the washer door shut. This action triggered a reaction—the front lower portion of the washer fell off onto my bare feet. The not "quite right" screws had popped out of the metal framework. The hard, cold piece of metal lying on my toes had exposed the cavernous opening under the washer. I chuckled as the leak repair job was exposed. There, all balled up and shoved within the inside of the under area of the washer was one of my favorite towels doing what towels do—soaking up water. Some things you cannot hide for long. The towel would only hold so much water and then it would be discovery time.

That same day I realized that the bathroom exhaust fan was not working. I brought in a stepping stool and climbed up to check out the problem. Guess what—another towel was the culprit. A mate to the one under the washer had been stuffed into the fan to stop any cold air from coming inside the bathroom. It looks to me like towels are almost as good as, or run a close second to, duct tape for almost any needed repair and should be included in mountain men tool boxes.

My Mountain Man makes me laugh. I love him and like to spoil him when I can. He loves pork chops and lots of ketchup. This dish is a favorite and I even let him put ketchup on it if he has to.

GARLIC PAPRIKA PORK CHOPS

Serves 4-6

4 pounds of pork chops
2 teaspoons salt
2 teaspoons black pepper
3 tablespoons butter
3 tablespoons olive oil
2 tablespoons sweet paprika
2 large yellow onions, finely chopped
½ cup tomato juice or one small can tomato paste mixed with ¼ cup water
1 cup sour cream
3 tablespoons all-purpose flour

Season the pork with salt and pepper. Set aside.

In a large sauté pan with a lid, over medium heat, combine the butter and oil. When the butter has melted, add the paprika and cook, stirring constantly for one minute.

Add the pork, cook until browned for 3-4 minutes per side. Transfer the pork to a plate and set aside.

Add the onion and sauté until softened about 4 minute. Stir in the tomato juice, then return the pork to the pan. Reduce the heat to low, cover and simmer until the pork is cooked through, about 40-50 minutes.

Transfer the pork to a serving platter and cover with foil to keep warm.

In a small bowl, mix together the sour cream and flour; then add the mixture to the liquid in the pan. Cook, stirring constantly, until the sauce thickens slightly; about 2-3 minutes. Spoon the tangy sauce and the pork over a heap of buttered egg noodles.

To serve, place a pork chops on a heap of buttered egg noodles. Spoon on the tangy sauce and serve extra sauce on the side.

MY MOST MEMORABLE CAKE

Helpful Hint: Before starting any baking project, it's a good idea to organize all the ingredients listed in a recipe. Line them up in the order they are called for before you actually start mixing. As you use an ingredient, set it aside. That way, nothing should be left on the work surface when you are through. A quick look during and after mixing will let you know if something was left out. All of that is just a good idea—it has nothing to with my cake.

Bubble, bubble, toil and trouble—oh yeah—lots of trouble…

If something goes wrong, it's not always your fault. Do I smell something burning? No, it can't be! My gourmet chocolate cake had only been in the oven 11 minutes but the smoke was billowing from the oven and out through the heat-minder burner on the stove top. Holy smoke! This is what I said, but not what I was thinking as with metal spatula in hand I'm scraping burning embers of cake from the oven floor. A similar recipe required two 9-inch round cake pans and that is what I used. The batter filled these pans to within ½-inch from the top. That's really full, I thought. I anticipated that recipe should make a low rise, dense and wonderfully moist cake.

This was my first try with this recipe. I had wanted something really special for my husband's 55th birthday. The batter, now closely resembling an eighth grade science experiment, continued to bubble out of the pans faster than I could scrape it up. Cookie sheets were used to catch the globs of batter as they dropped from the sides of the cake pans.

I couldn't keep up. The sides of the cake pans were totally covered in batter, which was burning too. The more I scraped, the more the batter oozed, dripped and burned everywhere. There were even a few sparks. Determined to salvage some portion of the cake, I continued scraping up the cake briquettes during the entire one hour bake cycle.

It was February, about 30 degrees, and snow was falling outside. All of the windows were open and the smoke alarm was blaring. The forest creatures think it's hunting season and my cat, Gracie, is running around the house with her ears sideways. The results of my efforts produced two layers of a very interesting smoked chocolate birthday cake.

Next time I will use three pans, or pay better attention to my research notes. I used two 9-in. x 1½-in. pans and should have used two 9-in. x 2-in. round cake pans. Oops!

MARY'S MEMORABLE CHOCOLATE CAKE

CAKE:

½ cup semi-sweet chocolate chips
1½ cups hot coffee
3 cups sugar
2½ cups all-purpose flour
1½ cups unsweetened cocoa powder
2 teaspoons baking soda
¾ teaspoon baking powder
1¼ teaspoon salt
3 large eggs
¾ cup vegetable oil
1½ cups buttermilk
1 teaspoon vanilla

Preheat oven to 300 degrees. Spray two 9-in. x 2-in. round cake pans with no-stick cooking spray. Line bottoms with rounds of parchment paper and spray again. Combine chocolate chips and hot coffee in a bowl. Let mixture stand, whisking occasionally, until chocolate is melted and mixture is smooth. Bring together sugar, flour, cocoa powder, baking soda, baking powder and salt in a large bowl and mix. Beat eggs in the bowl of an electric mixer until thick and yellow, about 3-5 minutes. Slowly add oil, buttermilk, vanilla and melted chocolate mixture to eggs, beating until combined well. Add dry ingredients and beat on medium speed until just combined well. Divide batter between pans and bake in middle of oven until a toothpick inserted in center comes out clean, 45-55 minutes.

ICING:

2 cups semi-sweet chocolate chips
1 cup heavy cream
2 tablespoons sugar
2 tablespoons light corn syrup
¼ cup butter

In a medium saucepan, whisk together the cream, sugar, and corn syrup. Bring to a boil over medium heat, whisking until sugar is dissolved. Remove pan from heat and add chocolate chips, whisking until chocolate is melted and mixture is smooth. Cut butter into 3 pieces and add to frosting, whisking until smooth. Transfer icing to a bowl and chill until spreadable, about 30 minutes. Spread icing between cake layers and over top and sides. Keep cake covered and chilled. Bring to room temperature before serving.

I'M READY FOR SUMMER – ARE YOU?

April 3 and there it is—my first indoor ant of the season. The task of early morning laundry has me once again picking up the wet towels off of the floor at the base of the washing machine (which by the way is obviously still leaking), so that I can put down dry towels. The little guy that I surprised was quick, but I was quicker—SWAP—and he's mine.

The next day was town day for necessary errands, placing an order for a new washer and dryer, and grocery shopping. At the grocery store I loaded my cart with tick spray, bug bombs, spider spray, wasp traps, mosquito repellant, every product made by Raid, a fly swatter for each hand, smoke sticks for the moles, ant traps, yard fogger, a snake bite kit, cream for poison ivy, band-aids, and a large jug of wine.

After eight seasons in the mountains, I was a veteran Mountain Woman, armed with the appropriate artillery and refreshment. Thusly prepared, I'm ready for it. Look out, because here comes summer…

Our part of the country is famous for its fresh vegetables and fruits from the gardens and orchards of the area. We have a preference for the ripe, red, juicy, and flavorful tomatoes. There is no comparison between the hot house grocery store tomato and one that you have just picked from the vine. As with all foods, fresh is best. You must try this!

NORTH WOODS FRESH TOMATO TART

This recipe is a lot of work. I only make it myself once or twice a year, so we savor every bite!
Serves 4

INGREDIENTS FOR CRUST:

1¼ cups all-purpose flour
1 tablespoon fresh thyme leaves (or 1 teaspoon dried)
½ teaspoon salt
Freshly ground black pepper, to taste
8 tablespoons cold, unsalted butter, cut into small pieces
2 teaspoons Dijon mustard
4 tablespoons ice water

INGREDIENTS FOR FILLING:

6 tablespoons olive oil
1 large onion, halved and slivered
2 each yellow and red bell peppers, cored, seeded and thinly sliced
1 tablespoon fresh thyme or 1 teaspoon dried
1 tablespoon fresh rosemary, chopped, or 1 teaspoon dried
Salt and freshly ground black pepper to taste
½ cup slivered fresh basil leaves
¼ cup chopped flat-leaf parsley
4 cloves garlic

INGREDIENTS FOR TOPPING:

1 cup grated fresh mozzarella cheese
2-3 ripe large tomatoes, cut into ¼-inch slices
¼ teaspoon freshly ground black pepper
2 tablespoons fresh thyme leaves
1 tablespoon chopped flat-leaf parsley
1 tablespoon extra-virgin olive oil

Prepare the pastry: Combine the flour, thyme, salt and pepper in a bowl. Add the butter and mix together with your fingertips or pastry cutter until the mixture resembles coarse meal. Stir in the mustard and enough ice water for the mixture to hold together. Form the dough into a thick disc.

Wrap in plastic wrap and chill in the refrigerator for at least 1 hour.

Meanwhile prepare the filling. Heat the oil in a large, heavy pot over medium-low heat. Add the onions, peppers, thyme, rosemary, salt, and pepper. Cook, uncovered stirring frequently, until the vegetables are cooked and the mixture resembles marmalade, at least 45 minutes.

Add the basil, parsley and garlic and continue stirring, 5 minutes. Adjust the seasonings. Drain the vegetables well, reserve.

Preheat the oven to 375 degrees.

On a lightly floured surface roll out the dough to form a 12-inch circle about 1/8-inch thick. Transfer to an 11-inch tart pan with a removable bottom, and press the pastry into the bottom and sides. Or just place dough on a baking sheet and form a ½-inch raised edge around the pastry. Prick the bottom of the crust with a fork and line with aluminum foil. Fill with dried beans to weight. Bake the crust for 10 minutes. Carefully remove the beans and foil and bake 10 minutes longer. Allow the crust to cool.

Spread the cheese over the bottom of the tart shell. Then spread the reserved filling over the cheese. Arrange the tomatoes overlapping in a circular pattern, to cover the surface. Sprinkle with pepper, thyme and parsley. Drizzle with olive oil.

Bake for 40 minutes. Let the tart rest for 10 minutes. To serve, carefully remove the side of the pan and run a thin spatula under the crust to loosen it from the bottom. If baked on a baking sheet, simply cut into wedges and serve. Top with fresh grated Parmesan or Pecorino Romano cheese. Place on a platter and serve hot or at room temperature.

BLUE TEETH

The funny dog with blue teeth—that's Mattie!

Mattie is always first in line at the start of the annual Easter egg hunt. She always finds the first and the most eggs. How does she do this? It is easy—she cheats. When you help to hide the eggs, as she does, it makes them much easier to find.

She is known around here as the famous black lab of the North Woods that loves blue Easter eggs. There she goes! There goes Mattie with another blue egg! This always creates squeals of delight from everyone, grandparents and children alike, better than even the Easter Bunny could. She carries her prize ever so gently. On command she will carefully drop the egg, completely intact with not even a crack, into your hand. The blue dye has however, left its mark on her lips, teeth, and tongue. Her beautiful blue grin always gives her secret away.

When allowed, Mattie will eagerly consume her wonderful egg. This creates an "afterburner effect" that is extremely powerful. Poor Mattie has to stay outside for awhile. No living creature wants to be within a mile radius of her. If she is in the house, the roof raises, the floor sinks, and the windows and doors open themselves.

As long as we're on the topic of eggs, the following recipe is outstanding and guaranteed not to turn your mouth blue. The dish is very tasty and the presentation is elegant.

FANCY EGGS IN PUFF PASTRY

Serves 8

8 commercially frozen puff pastry patty shells
¼ cup plus 2 tablespoons butter, divided
¼ pound fresh mushrooms, sliced
6 spears fresh asparagus, cut into 1-inch pieces
3 tablespoons all-purpose flour
1½ cups milk
¾ teaspoon salt
¼ teaspoon pepper
6 eggs
¼ cup half and half
¼ teaspoon ground red pepper
1 tablespoon butter
¾ cup shredded Cheddar cheese

Bake patty shells according to package directions; set aside. Melt 2 tablespoons butter in a large skillet. Add mushrooms and asparagus; sauté until tender. Set aside.

Melt ¼ cup butter in a heavy saucepan over low heat; add flour, stirring until smooth. Cook 1 minute, stirring constantly. Gradually add milk; cook over medium heat, stirring constantly, until mixture is thickened and bubbly. Stir in salt and pepper. Cover and set aside.

Combine eggs, half-and-half, and red pepper, stir well with a wire whisk. Melt 1 tablespoon butter in a large skillet over medium heat. Add egg mixture. Cook over medium-low heat, stirring gently, until cooked but still creamy. Stir in sautéed vegetables and white sauce.

Place patty shells on a baking sheet. Spoon egg mixture into patty shells, and sprinkle with cheese. Broil 6 inches from heat 30 seconds or until cheese melts. Serve immediately.

SPECIAL TIMES

Power outages are a frequent happening. The usual causes are snow, ice, breaking tree branches from wind, rain and lightning storms. Occasionally an animal or a car sliding out of control will damage a power pole or lines. We do have a generator for use in such circumstances. We aren't always in a hurry to fire up the generator however. We light candles, prepare some cold snacks and just enjoy the forced inactivity and quiet conversation. However, one must remember that without power, water won't flow and toilets won't flush.

We seem to have such busy days that there is not the time there once was to just sit and watch. Together we are learning that we have to make those times happen. When you take time to sit and enjoy the moment, there is no better place than this. The garden, of course, is a lovely place to sit and enjoy the hummingbirds and the flowers. Another favorite place is the wood swing by the river. Armed with a simple plate of apples, cheese and crackers we are as happy as if it was filet mignon.

A glass of Champagne, my husband at my side, and my arms are full of roses from the grocery store because I can't grow my own as we walk hand in hand to the bridge. The silver glow of the moon is on the water and we do indeed feel lucky. It has become our magical mountain hide-a-way. It doesn't get any better than this.

The mountains have become a place for imagination and a place to play. David not only lights the bridge for Christmas. There are red and white lights for Valentine's Day and a large heart. There are green lights for St. Patrick's Day and red, white and blue for the 4th of July.

Some of our most special times are spent in the kitchen cooking dinner together and chatting about the day, the dog, the cat, or the neighbors.

One particular recipe stands out in my mind, fish tacos. This was a totally new approach to tacos for me. We've had beef, chicken and turkey tacos, but never fish. They really didn't sound good to me, but rumor had it they were quite tasty. So it was back to the lab and some research. The results is the ultimately perfectly delicious fish taco. You just can't stop at one or two. Sometimes you pray for just one huge burp so that you can squeeze in just one more taco. So here we go. I did the research. If you follow my recipe you will award me the Nobel Peace Prize or the James Beard Award or an Academy Award or some old soccer trophy you've had in the closet for the last 16 years gathering dust. Bon Appétit!

NORTH WOODS FISH TACOS
OR
EAGLE DROP LEFT OVERS

I like halibut or cod but occasionally the neighborhood bald eagle drops his prey after fishing the river. If you're on the ball, you could take his fish—but run fast because he will want it back!

Serves 4, but on a hungry night, the two of us can finish it off!

1 mango, peeled, pitted, and cut into 1/3-inch cubes
1 firm, ripe avocado, peeled, pitted, and cut into 1/3-inch cubes
2 scallions or green onions thinly sliced
½ cup coarsely chopped cilantro leaves
2 tablespoons fresh lime juice, plus wedges for serving
1¾ teaspoons Kosher salt—divided
3 tablespoons cornmeal
1 teaspoon cumin
1 teaspoon chili powder
1 pound white fish
4 tablespoons vegetable oil
16 six-inch corn tortillas
2 jalapeño peppers, halved, ribs and seeds discarded, thinly sliced.
Hot sauce or taco sauce optional

Place mango, avocado, scallion, juice and ½ teaspoon salt in a bowl. Toss gently, for salsa and set aside. Combine cornmeal, cumin, chili powder and remaining 1¼ teaspoon salt in a bowl; add fish and toss until coated well, discard excess coating and set aside.

Using 2 tablespoons oil, lightly brush onto one side of each tortilla. Heat a large nonstick skillet over moderately high heat add tortillas in pairs with uncoated sides together and cook, turning once, until just golden and starting to crisp, 2-4 minutes. Transfer to a plate and cover with a towel, or place in a taco shell warmer dish.

Heat remaining 2 tablespoons oil in same skillet, add jalapeño and fish; toss to coat with oil. Cook, stirring occasionally, until fish is just cooked through, 4 to 5 minutes. Spoon into paired taco shells. Serve with salsa, lime wedges and hot sauce, if desired.

MEAN MOTHER NATURE

Mother Nature can play cruel jokes. After a long winter, the coming of spring makes us all a little giddy. Spring fever hits as daffodils push through the just thawed ground. We start reading seed catalogues and planning gardens. As soon as the weather is nice enough to have the windows open I jump into spring cleaning. When the cleaning bug bites, there is nothing left untouched. From the chandeliers to the back corners of the closets everything is moved, polished, cleaned, and scrubbed. My first spring cleaning at the cabin went well. It was an absolutely beautiful day and the windows were open wide, all twenty of them. There was just a slight breeze and the house was so clean and fresh.

The yellow haze descending upon us was silent and thorough. It sifted through the screens on the open windows settling on every square inch of everything. The yellow dust rested on the couches, tables, chairs, television, plants, computer, paperwork, and on top of the refrigerator. It was even under the stove. I couldn't shut the windows fast enough.

The discovery of pine pollen was in itself a nightmare. Every Spring the pine trees dump massive clouds of golden-yellow pollen into the air. If you have allergies, you go to town for a month. When Spring rains come, there are yellow mud pies wherever the pollen has been washed from roofs, cars or anything else that is outside and coated with the dust. The wind causes great yellow swirls of dancing pollen as it blows from tree branches. I have learned my lesson. No matter how nice the day, my windows are never open in the Spring.

After such a hard day at home, I needed comfort food. And, as I mentioned earlier on, my most comforting comfort food is pasta. The following recipe is perfect for a Spring dinner.

SPRING FLING PASTA

Serves 4

1 pound fresh fettuccine pasta
¼ cup virgin olive oil
3 tablespoons minced garlic
½ teaspoon dried red pepper flakes
2 teaspoons grated lemon zest
2 cups dry white wine
2 tablespoons fresh lemon juice
1 pound fresh or frozen Dungeness crab leg and body meat
2 cups fresh asparagus, cut in 2-in. diagonal strips, lightly steamed
4 tablespoons mixed, chopped fresh herbs such as chives, basil, thyme, marjoram, parsley and tarragon
Salt and pepper to taste
1½ cups freshly shredded Parmesan cheese

In a very large saucepan or stockpot, bring a large amount of lightly salted water to a boil and cook the fettuccine until al dente, then drain.

Meanwhile, in another large saucepan, heat the olive oil over medium heat and cook the garlic, red pepper flakes and lemon zest, stirring often for 3-4 minutes. Add the white wine and lemon juice, bring to a gentle boil, and cook to reduce the liquid volume by half.

Add the drained, cooked pasta, crab, asparagus, and chopped fresh herbs to the pan. Cook, stirring gently , until the ingredients are just heated through, about 3-4 minutes. Add salt and pepper, if necessary.

Serve immediately, sprinkled with Parmesan cheese and garnish with lemon wedges and herb sprigs. Serves 4.

THE FRIGHTENED FAWN

There are some events in the course of a lifetime that are sweet, wonderful, and totally unforgettable. I would like to share one of my unforgettable moments with you.

I was about 2 miles from home, returning from an early morning walk when a small, red car sped by me and suddenly pulled off the road and came to a stop. I stood still not knowing what to expect. Was someone going to grab me off the road and stuff me in their trunk? Did they stop for monkey business, dirty business, or what? As it turned out, the stop was for doggie business. The lady that emerged from this little red car opened the back door and four huge dogs came bounding out to take care of "business". That was OK.

I continued on. It was a winding mountain road and around the next bend was a special surprise. A deer was standing in the road looking down at a what appeared to be a small animal at her feet. I feared that her baby had been hit by a car. Just then an old pick-up truck whizzed by and the mother bounded away into the thickets. Afraid of what I would find, I approached the animal on the road. I had to walk past anyway to get home.

The soft brown eyes that looked up at me from under long lashes were in a sweet little face that appeared to be surrounded by a coil of very long, skinny legs. The ears were oversized and its light brown body was dotted with creamy white spots. I had never been this close to a fawn before.

A second car whizzed by and the frightened fawn cried out. If you stepped on the big toe of a sheep, that is the sound you would hear. This baby had good lungs. As I talked softly to him in an attempt to calm and quiet his fear, he responded with kitten-like mews. We were actually communicating, well kind of. The mother had returned and was standing in a near-by meadow watching. It was time for me to go.

Not wanting to leave and end this special moment but knowing that I had to, I turned and started the last leg of my walk home. There was a rustling behind me. My fawn had stood and taken his first steps and was preparing to follow me. It was awesome, but wrong. Clapping my hands and making swinging arm motions I guided him away from the road and into the thicket. Mama was there waiting for him.

The events of this day had left a lifetime footprint in my mind. I wanted a special meal that night to go along with the special story I had to tell David when he got home. So I stirred up an all-time favorite. It takes some time, but it's worth the effort.

CHICKEN WITH HERBED DUMPLINGS

Serves 6-8

INGREDIENTS FOR CHICKEN:

1 whole roasting chicken, about 4-5 pounds, cut into 6 pieces
1 onion, coarsely chopped
2 celery stalks
4 bay leaves
2 tablespoons black peppercorns
2 tablespoons chopped fresh thyme, or 1 tablespoon dried
4 whole cloves
Pinch of saffron (optional)
6 garlic cloves, crushed
1 cup dry white wine
8 cups water
2/3 cup butter
1 cup all-purpose flour
1 cup fresh or thawed frozen pearl onions
2 carrots, peeled and cut into ¼-inch rounds
4 cups shelled peas
Salt and pepper to taste
Chopped fresh parsley (optional)

Rinse the cut chicken pieces in cold water and drain. Place the chicken in a large pot with the chopped onion, celery, herbs, spices, garlic, wine and water. Cover, bring to a low simmer over medium heat and cook until the chicken meat falls away from the bones, 2 to 2 ½ hours.

Remove from the heat and drain, reserving the stock. Let the chicken cool, then pull the meat from the bones, discarding the bones and skin.

Melt the butter in a large, heavy pot or Dutch oven over low heat. Gradually whisk in the flour until thoroughly blended and cook until golden (5-10 minutes) stirring frequently to avoid scorching. Remove the fat from the reserved chicken stock and whisk the stock into the flour-butter mixture, whisking between additions to avoid lumps. Cook at a low simmer until thickened, stirring frequently and skimming off any fat or foam that rises to the surface. Add the onions, carrots peas, and chicken. Reduce to a simmer and season with salt and pepper.

INGREDIENTS FOR DUMPLINGS:

- 2 cups all-purpose flour
- 1 tablespoon baking powder
- 1 teaspoon sugar
- ½ teaspoon salt
- ¼ cup minced onion
- ½ teaspoon celery seeds
- 1 tablespoon chopped fresh sage or 1 teaspoon dried
- 4 tablespoons chopped fresh parsley
- 1 cup milk

In a large bowl, mix the dumpling ingredients thoroughly to make a thick batter. If necessary, add water to the batter. Scoop the batter into large tablespoonfuls and drop into the simmering liquid. Cover and cook the dumplings for 15-20 minutes, or until puffy and cooked through.

Serve in large bowls, garnish with chopped parsley.

MARY'S NORTH WOODS HERB GARDEN

I have discovered that certain herbs grow very well in my north woods garden. The following herbs are good choices to create a basic garden of herbs that will add flavor and excitement to a large variety of home-cooked dishes. They have the best flavor when grown with bright sun and minimal water once established.

Don't be afraid to experiment with them. A little nibble of the fresh herb tells you a lot about it. If the flavor is mild straight from the plant, you can use substantial quantities. But if it tastes like you have bitten into a handful of pine needles, use it with discretion.

BASIL: There are many varieties of basil. My favorite is the green leafed sweet basil. There is an intense taste that is great for pesto, pastas and salads. It thrives in warm, hot weather and does well in pots. The attractive flower heads with their tiny white flowers can be torn apart and sprinkled in salads or used as a garnish. At any rate, you should deadhead the basil so that it doesn't go to seed. The plant will produce longer. Our growing season is short, so purchasing established plants works better than starting plants from seed.

CHIVES: This relative of the onion has a mild onion flavor. Use it as a garnish, or minced to use in salads, cheese, egg dishes, and soups. The plants make an attractive edging for flower beds and can be used in pots. They have rose-purple flowers that can be torn apart and sprinkled as garnishes in salads and soups. The flower petals are a lot stronger in flavor and fragrance than the leaves.

OREGANO: Known as the pizza herb, oregano is also used in many Italian tomato-based dishes. Use it to season meats, salads, vinegars, casseroles, and breads. It is a very hardy and easy to grow perennial. My favorite is the Greek. It has great flavor and the flowers are a pretty purple. Another attractive variety for the garden is the golden creeping oregano. A relative of the oregano is marjoram (actually wild oregano). Some prefer its milder flavor.

PARSLEY: You can't use too much parsley. Whether you prefer Italian flat leaf or the curly version, the fresh grassy flavor compliments most foods. Use it to flavor soups, sauté it lightly to season vegetables, mince it and sprinkle it fresh on casseroles and salads. It's great with poultry, pastas and breads. The curly (French) makes a very attractive garnish. For a stronger flavor and one that holds up in cooking, use the Italian. I take the scissors and cut off bunches at a time for use. You could snip just a sprig here and there. When the leaves become tough and sparse, let the plant go to seed and self-sow or replant. Parsley plants are usually only good for two seasons.

ROSEMARY: Known as the herb of welcome, the strong, pungent plant flavor of this herb compliments lamb, poultry, and veal. It is fantastic in marinades for beef and for use in vinegars. In milder climates, it is used a lot in landscaping. They can grow into quite large shrubs and most varieties have attractive little blue flowers. I grow my rosemary in pots in the garden so that I can bring them inside to winter over. They are kept in the root cellar and only given a little water about once a month. In the Spring, outside they go after a little hardening up. It's nice to have a pot by the door and as you walk by, brush your hand through it to release the wonderful fragrance.

SAGE: This powerfully flavored herb is most thought of in terms of turkey dressing at Thanksgiving. It is also used for pork and beef. Golden and purple sage are pretty for the garden, but for the classic flavor, use garden sage. Large sage leaves make a unique appetizer when briefly fried in olive oil, drained on a paper towel, and sprinkled with salt. A real delicacy is the blue sage flowers. They are filled with a sweet nectar and are delicious on salads or to use as a garnish on appetizer plates. I like to pick them and suck the nectar out. You will never find these flowers at the market. You have to grow your own. The plants are very hardy and winter over outside even in the northern climates.

THYME: These aromatic leaves give a tang to fish, soups, and vegetables. Plants grow as a hardy ground cover that you can walk on or as small shrubs. They are great for rock gardens. In the spring they have little pink flowers. Like most herbs, they are drought tolerant. Fresh thyme is a nice additive to salads, vinaigrettes, marinades,

Italian dishes and breads. The lemon thyme is excellent with fish and salads.

I grow all of these herbs and more in my north woods garden. To me, herbs are nothing short of magic. They grow easily, have flowers, have mouth watering aromas, and are attractive to birds and butterflies as well as humans. They are the magic ingredients that enhance the taste of most of the food and drink that we consume. There are so many of these beautiful and fragrant plants. I am asked all the time, "What do you do with them?" My answer would fill another book. It would be easier to say "What can't you do with them?"

Here is one tasty and very pretty suggestion: a summer salad with a simple vinaigrette.

SUMMER SALAD

Mixed salad greens such as lettuce, sorrel, and young spinach
Edible flowers such as nasturtiums, borage, violets, and Johnny jump-ups
Leaves of nasturtiums have a peppery taste and can be added as well.

Make the basis of the salad from a mixture of variously colored and shaped salad leaves, toss in a handful of edible flowers and leaves. The blue borage provides a lovely color contrast to the nasturtiums. Sage flowers are sweet and a fun additive. Add fresh herbs according to taste (chives, parsley, cilantro, basil, or mint, to name a few). Make just a simple vinaigrette dressing. Just before serving, toss with the salad in a large serving bowl. This is an exciting and delicious salad.

SIMPLE VINAIGRETTE

Makes 1 cup

¼ cup red wine vinegar
2 tablespoons balsamic vinegar
1 tablespoon chopped shallot
2 teaspoons Dijon mustard
½ teaspoon salt
Freshly ground black pepper to taste
¾ cup extra-virgin olive oil

Puree all the ingredients except the oil in a food processor. With the machine running, pour in the olive oil in a steady stream. It will keep for several weeks in the refrigerator. Bring to room temperature and shake before using.

AMAZING AUNT PEARL

Our mountain soil has grown Dad's garden full of blueberries and my herbs have flourished. I have only recently learned that this area was also home to a world renowned bonsai business. The founders of this business lived a part of their lives in my parents green house, which is now my gift shop (more about that later).

A good friend of mine lives in the cabin just down the lane from me. Her name is Penny and she lives in what used to be Aunt Pearl's cabin and she has shared her aunt's story with me.

Aunt Pearl lived in what is now Penny's cabin after her second husband died. Her son Jim and his wife Louisa lived in what is now my gift shop cabin. Pearl left her home in Deer Cove at age 93 to live in a nursing home. (She had some kind of cancer.) She was born and raised in the Sunnyside area and had many brothers and sisters. As a young woman, she hunted game on horseback in the hills where we live now in order to help feed her siblings.

She married a Japanese-American high school classmate soon after graduating. He was the only Japanese-American living in the area and suffered greatly from his classmates' taunts and abuses. He went by the name of Kelly. It was given to him by his classmates after one of them had dumped a bucket of green paint on him as a prank. Shortly after he and Pearl, Penny's great aunt, were married, he told her that the only reason he married her was to "get even" with the whites.

Pearl was stuck in a loveless, and probably abusive, relationship, but because she came from a devout Catholic family, divorce was not an option. They went on to have two sons together and developed a nursery business that was nationally renowned for bonsai.

At the start of World War II, when anti-Japanese sentiment was high and Japanese-Americans were being forced into internment camps, government officials came to take away her husband and sons. They took away her husband and oldest son (Jim), but she refused to let them take her youngest son, Sam. She threatened them with a shotgun if they tried to take him, and they left him with her. He had been crippled as a child in an accident.

Pearl waited faithfully for her husband to be released from the camp and also ran the family nursery business. Shortly after his release from the camp, he told her he wanted a divorce and though she tried to dissuade him (because of her faith), he was adamant and so they were divorced. She went on to remarry. Her oldest son ran the family nursery business for many years until he finally sold it.

I never got to meet Pearl, but I'm told that she was an amazing, kind, courageous, and hardworking woman. She always kept a positive attitude and was a light and inspiration in many people's lives.

The following is a zucchini bread recipe that Pearl gave to Penny and Penny is now sharing with us. This recipe is as amazing as Aunt Pearl was.

AUNT PEARL'S MAUNA KEA ZUCCHINI BREAD

Beat until creamy:

- 2 cups white cane sugar
- 3 eggs
- 1 cup vegetable oil
- 2 teaspoons vanilla
- 2 teaspoons freshly grated orange peel

Add:

- 2 cups grated zucchini
- 1 cup well-drained crushed pineapple

Mix well.

Sift together:

- 3 cups white all-purpose flour
- 1 teaspoon salt
- 2 teaspoons soda
- ½ teaspoon baking powder
- 1½ teaspoons cinnamon
- ¼ teaspoon cloves
- ¼ teaspoon allspice

Pearl would sift all of the dry ingredients together twice.

Stir in:

- 1 cup pecans or walnuts, chopped
- 1 cup golden raisins
- ½ cup dates

Fold nut/flour mixture into the zucchini mixture. Pour into two 9 x 5-inch greased and floured loaf pans. Bake at 350 for one hour or until toothpick in center comes out clean.

SNAKE JUMPING: NOT AN OLYMPIC SPORT!

How high can you jump? You don't want to learn this the way that I did. One sunny afternoon, as I was leaving Mom and Dad's house, I turned to wave and say good-bye and nearly tripped over a coiled rattlesnake. I saw movement out of the corner of my eye, heard the rattle, and managed to jump over the snake. I'm sure I was airborne by two feet. I screamed for David. The dogs were very curious and excited. They had never seen me jump before! I could not leave the scene for fear that the snake would strike at my dogs. So there I am—saying good-bye to my parents, flapping my arms to keep the dogs away from the snake, and impatiently waiting for my husband to bring a snake-killing instrument and rescue me. Finally he heard me, came around the corner, quickly assessed the situation and took care of the snake. My Hero!

There was one afternoon when it was my turn to come around the corner and save him. It's not often that I get to be the hero. He was standing beside our car that was parked in front of the house. When I came around the bend of the lane to the house, there he was with two rattlesnakes coiled at his feet. He had not noticed either one. (They don't make much noise until they feel threatened. I think they liked him.) Anyway, I yelled at him, he jumped and the snakes started to slither slowly away. They were literally wrapped up in themselves involved in a little fatal attraction and easy to do away with.

My first snake kill was the hardest. The reptile was coiled at the corner of the house. Once again my dogs, Mattie and Cookie, were there. I heard the snake's warning rattles and hisses before I saw it. Sometimes I'm in such a hurry that I forget to be careful, and I know better. In the summer months, snakes are a constant worry. When I yelled "Kennel Up," my dogs obediently responded and turned to go to their kennel.

Feeling absolutely terrified and shaking, I ran for the shovel. I just kept telling myself that I could do this, yes, I could do this. Knowing that snakes can jump the length of their bodies, I knew that my shovel handle was way too short. With my hands shaking, I took a lunge at the snake with the shovel and harpooned the side of my house. The gouge in the cedar will always remind me of my first kill. Of course I totally missed the snake on my first try. I made a second try and chopped its head off. (Oh, that is so gross!) The head with about 2 inches of body went dancing across the parking area and the rest of the snake writhed around on the ground at my feet. I went after the head part and whacked again yelling "Fore" as I sent it flying. I put my 7-iron down (it looked a lot like a shovel) and went to retrieve the head. It had to be carefully disposed of because the venom stays active even though the snake is dead.

We have timber rattlesnakes and diamondback rattlesnakes as well as many varieties of harmless snakes. The rattlesnake can exceed 7 feet long and is also referred to as a pit viper. It has a spade shaped head, a fiendish fang and venom system and heat sensing facial pits. It has reserve fangs to replace any which break off in a victim. The venom causes extensive tissue damage, bleeding, and swelling in humans and a bite can be fatal. The facial pits, in effect, infrared detectors, guide the snake swiftly and surely to warm blooded prey such as rodents and humans.

The rattler will coil, rattle fearsomely, and stand its ground when threatened. It bites hundreds of people a year, more than any other venomous snake in the United States. It usually hunts at night. It ambushes victims along their trails or attacks them in beds and burrows.

Keep in mind that snakes can swim. Yes, the snake can swim quite nicely, holding its rattles above the water to keep them dry.

The young are born complete with fangs and venom, armed and dangerous at birth. These snakes hibernate for the winter and emerge in spring hungry and mean. They can live for more than 20 years. Which, in my opinion, is way too long. (Portions of this information came from an article by Jay W. Sharp.)

So that there is no confusion, at this time, I must admit that I've become meaner than the snakes and I will win! All of this outside activity made me really hungry and not for snake or chicken. This Mountain Woman had a he-man appetite and wanted red meat!

So, I poured myself a glass of Cabernet and went to the garden in search of some fresh basil, parsley, rosemary, and thyme. This is the steak to eat after you jump snakes or whack their heads off. It gives you something to look forward to!

STEAK FOR PROUD MARY!
SIRLOIN STEAK STUFFED WITH FRESH BASIL

Serves 6-8

1 boneless sirloin steak (2½ pounds and 1½-inches thick)
½ teaspoon salt
¼ teaspoon black pepper
¼ cup minced fresh parsley
1½ cups lightly packed fresh basil
¼ cup finely chopped onion
4 garlic cloves minced
1-2 teaspoons fresh rosemary, minced (I like lots of rosemary and use more)
½ teaspoon fresh thyme
1 teaspoon olive oil

Using a sharp knife, make 5 lengthwise cuts three-fourths of the way through the steak to resemble pockets. Combine salt, pepper and parsley; rub over steak.

Coarsely chop the basil; add onion, garlic, rosemary and thyme. Stuff into pockets in steak. Use heavy-duty string, tie the steak at 2-inch intervals, closing the pockets.

Drizzle with oil. Grill, covered, over indirect medium heat for 35-45 minutes or until the meat reaches desired doneness. Cover and let stand for 5-10 minutes. Remove string before slicing.

THE HAPPY HOUR SNAKE

August 17, 2007, was hot. The day's high had been 102 degrees. After putting in an eleven hour day at the auto repair business, it was good to get home, fix something refreshing to drink and go sit by the river. Finding that I had no soda in the house, I went over to the guest house (better known as Warehouse 13). The place also served as an extra pantry for the over-flow of "stuff" that I couldn't seem to make room for in the house.

As I stepped outside onto the wood planking of the deck at the back of the house, I had just a moment to think to myself how lucky I was to live in such beautiful surroundings. Suddenly I froze in one spot as I became aware of the undeniable sound of a rattlesnake. The rattling was loud and very, very close. I could hear it, but I couldn't see it. Every hair on my body was standing on end.

Looking down, I could see that the snake was not at my feet or between me and the back door. When I moved to go inside, the rattling became louder. "David, you've got to hear this," I whispered. (Didn't want the snake to know that I was calling for reinforcements.)

Together we found it. As it turned out the snake was only a few feet from us. It had become stuck in a live-trap that we kept under a work table. The same one that we used to trap and relocate the gray diggers. David took the dogs to kennel-up so they wouldn't be helpful. He came back to the deck with a shovel, a small garden rake and two dogs. In his haste, he had forgotten to shut the gate to the kennel. So I retraced his steps and took the dogs to the kennel. Meanwhile, he analyzed the situation at hand.

When I returned to the deck, he was gingerly reaching under the table to move the trap forward. The snake suddenly freed itself and began striking at him! Instantly, I headed for the top of the patio table. Fiercely, David attacked the snake with the shovel, repeatedly attempting to chop its head off. Finally, he succeeded in killing it. The severed head was hissing and snapping and the body was writhing on the bloody deck timbers. My hero, standing in a pool of rattlesnake blood, inspects his shovel and says "Hmm. I guess I should sharpen this."

We cleaned up the mess with the garden hose and carefully disposed of the carcass in the garbage can. Finally, with refreshments in hand, we did walk to the river, watching the ground every step of the way. Incidentally, this snake that showed up for Happy Hour was a small one. It had eight rattles and was only about two feet long. But trust me, it was big enough!

That night we had a simple dinner of crab sandwiches and a green salad. We ate outside, but not on the deck. We chose a table by the river.

These sandwiches are delicious, but now they always remind me of the Happy Hour Snake so I have named them The Happy Hour Crab Sandwiches.

THE HAPPY HOUR CRAB SANDWICHES

Serves 2

8 ounces of Dungeness crab meat, fresh or frozen
2 teaspoons fresh lemon juice
2 tablespoons minced fresh chives or minced green onions
2 tablespoons minced red bell pepper
2 tablespoons minced celery
4 ounces cream cheese at room temperature
½ teaspoon Dijon mustard
½ cup grated sharp cheddar cheese
Salt and pepper to taste
2 French rolls, or whatever kind you like, split in half

In a bowl, place the crab meat and sprinkle with the lemon juice.

Add the chives or onion, bell pepper, celery, cream cheese, mustard, half the cheddar, salt and pepper, and mix well.

Divide the crab meat mixture among the rolls and top with the remaining cheddar. Place under a broiler until heated through and cheese is bubbly.

CHEERS!

TAKE A HIKE!

Go ahead, I dare ya. Take a hike. Just be aware and remember your place—the mountains of the Wenatchee National Forest.

The first thing to do prior to your hike is to dress appropriately. Graffiti is bad when seen on the sides of buildings and fences, but even worse when you are viewing it on your arms and legs. I learned the hard way to protect my skin from the graffiti capabilities of flying, stinging, biting and crawling insects. Another area of concern would be the thorns, branches, and pollens of the various aggressive vegetative matter that abounds in the forest. Sometimes these plants seem to be alive as they reach out for you as you pass by.

The rocks not only give you something to trip over or create an obstacle for you to climb over, but they also hide snakes and other creatures that are more than willing to leave their mark on you. After one expensive visit to the doctor due to red, raised, swirly bumps on my legs from contact with some kind of plant material (we think), I now cover up.

When we lived in town, I frequented the gym 3-4 days a week. That activity is no longer feasible. Now, as schedule permits, a 3-6 mile hike takes the place of the machinery that used to make my muscles complain. The scenery of Chinook Pass by far surpasses the sweating bodies and painted walls of the work-out room. So do the raccoons.

My first encounter with a raccoon happened as I was walking along soaking up a beautiful morning. It was between 5:30 and 6:00 AM as I went striding along and deeply inhaling the fresh mountain air. Movement in the road up ahead caught my eye. I was still too far away to make out what the object was so I continued walking and watching. A dog, I thought. It had to be a dog. As I closed the gap between us, I could see that it was no dog. It was big and hairy, but not a dog.

At a distance of about 20 feet an absolutely huge raccoon raised up on its back legs and waved at me, sort of. He appeared to be about four feet tall and vicious. He was walking toward me and hissing and spitting. I backed up.

If I ran, would he chase me? If I stayed put, would he eat me? Tree climbing—out of the question. I knew which of us would win that contest. Thank goodness, Mr. Raccoon decided that I was not worth the effort and ambled off the road and up the nearest tree to warily watch me walk by.

This tasty and easy recipe is a special treat for brunch, breakfast, or an afternoon snack. Especially wonderful after a hike in the North Woods.

BANAPPLE BREAD

A Scrumptious Snack for the Hiker

3 eggs
1 cup salad oil
2 cups granulated sugar
1 cup mashed bananas*
1 cup applesauce*
3 teaspoons pure vanilla
3 teaspoons ground cinnamon
1 teaspoon soda
1 teaspoon salt
3 cups all-purpose flour
½ teaspoon baking powder
½-1 cup walnuts or pecans, lightly toasted and broken into pieces (optional)
½ cup dark or golden raisins

Whip eggs until foamy. Mix banana, applesauce, oil, sugar and vanilla. Blend well. In a large bowl mix together flour, cinnamon, soda, salt and baking powder. Add to banana mixture and blend. Stir in nuts.

Lightly grease and flour two 9-inch loaf pans. Divide batter equally into the pans. Bake for 1 hour at 325 degrees.

**Note: You could also use 2 cups of bananas, pumpkin, zucchini, or carrots.*

AIN'T MISBEHAVIN' — JUST BEING MYSELF

Just when I think that finally, after years in the cabin, that the house is critter-proofed against the unwanted, there it is. A lizard in my kitchen. The jungle hop I did while watching it run across the floor was close to panic. Where were my cats? They could catch it. I had to act fast or it would be loose in the house and I would have to move.

Clubbing it on the head seemed too drastic. I needed a glove. I had to pick it up—oh yuck! Rummaging in the mud room with one eye on the lizard was productive. One gardening glove with a hole in it would have to do. Swooping, with gloved hand, I grabbed the six-inch monster. It was soft, kind of squishy, and wiggling in my hand. I just hoped it wouldn't touch the part of the glove with the hole before I could throw it outside. But of course, it did—oooooh!

I was at the back door in a heartbeat, threw it open and OUT the lizard went onto the deck and away. The lizard didn't mean to be bad. He was just being himself. Score: Mountain Woman "1", Lizard "0".

The last thing you expect at a BBQ with your parents is the presentation of a dead, dehydrated frog. We had just finished a lovely meal on the deck (the same one I threw the lizard out on). I was serving a dessert of fresh blueberry-nut loaf cake and ice cream and suddenly dangling in front of my face is exactly that—a dead frog. My husband, proudly holding his prize says, "Look what I found in the fridge hanging by one leg."

The referred to fridge was an outdoor mini refrigerator. Apparently, when some thirsty person had reached in for a beverage, this poor little guy had hopped in and that was that. The frog was gross, hanging about two inches from my face, and not even a little bit appreciated. My eyes had to cross to look at it. David thought it was just the neatest thing. I gave him the "look" and the frog went away. My husband didn't mean to be bad. He was just being himself. Score: Mountain Woman "2", Husband "0".

I must admit that the lizard and my husband with the frog both annoyed me. However, the blueberry-nut loaf cake was great. This is a delicate orange-flavored loaf, loaded with fresh blueberries and walnuts. It is delicious as a dessert or as a coffee cake. When you cut into it you will see the darker purple and magenta berries against a lighter, glowing orange background of cake. Gorgeous!

BLUEBERRY-NUT LOAF CAKE

Serves 10

1 ¼ cups fresh blueberries
2 cups sifted all-purpose flour
½ teaspoon salt
⅔ cup granulated sugar
1 ½ teaspoons baking powder
½ teaspoon baking soda
1 egg
2 tablespoons unsalted butter, melted
¾ cup orange juice (grate the rinds of 2 oranges before squeezing the juice)
Finely grated rind of 2 large, deep-colored oranges
1 ¼ cups walnuts or pecan halves or large pieces

Adjust a rack one-third up from the bottom of the oven and preheat to 350 degrees. Lightly grease a 10 ½ x 4 x 3-inch loaf pan. Line the pan with parchment paper. Butter the paper and dust it all with fine, dry bread crumbs, then—over a piece of paper—tap to shake out the excess crumbs. Set the pan aside.

Wash the berries in a large bowl of cold water. Then spread them out on a towel. Pat the tops lightly with paper towels and let stand until dry—the berries must be completely dry.

Place the dry berries in a bowl. Measure out the flour, then remove 1 teaspoon and toss the teaspoon of flour very gently on the berries. Set aside.

Sift together the remaining flour, salt, sugar, baking powder and baking soda. Set aside.

In the large bowl of an electric mixer, beat the egg just to mix. Mix in the butter and orange juice. Then on low speed, add the sifted dry ingredients and beat only to mix. Remove from the mixer.

Stir in the grated rind and then the nuts.

Spread about one-quarter of the mixture in the prepared pan—it will be a very thin layer.

Gently and carefully (without squashing) fold the floured berries into the remaining batter. Place over the thin layer in the pan.

Smooth the top.

Bake for 70 minutes, until a cake tester gently inserted into the middle comes out clean and dry. The cake will form a crack on the top during baking. It is supposed to. It looks beautiful.

Let the cake cool in the pan on a rack for about 10 minutes—but no longer, or it will steam and the bottom crust will be wet.

This is a tender and fragile cake—be extremely careful when you remove it from the pan. This is the reason for using parchment paper. Take hold of the parchment paper by the sides and gently raise the cake from the pan. After the cake has cooled, remove the paper.

THIS IS MARY'S PLACE, TOO

You're so close to the end, but hang on. It's confession time. Hard as it is for me to admit it—I have "caved". Yes, before God and country, the mice, spiders, and snakes, I willingly make this announcement—I HAVE CAVED! I started feeling this way after about five years of mountain life. Now after ten years, there is no doubt. David's mountain living dream and hide-a-way has become my dream also — Mary's Place.

Everywhere you look, even under the rocks, you will find me or something I have planted, grown or killed. My kitchen is filled with bits and pieces of antiquity that I have found and hung on nails from the cross beams. The great room of our home has lace curtains with a pinecone motif on all of the windows. I've diligently made my mark in the North Woods.

The hummingbirds come back to us in March and I make sure that their feeders are filled to the brim with red, sweet nectar to entice the quick, shimmering bits of winged fluorescent color. I maintain these feeders until September when the hummers need to begin their flight back to Mexico.

As I sit writing these notes, there are six of them zipping in, out and around their hanging dinner plates. They feed, zip and chirp-chatter as if playing a game with no rules. The cocktail I have poured for them today must be the "best batch ever".

There is a flag of pink and blue butterflies hanging suspended from the front gable of the sleeping loft. The deck at the rear of the house has six half wine barrels that look like goblins with piles of snow forming huge white domes over them during the winter months. These same barrel planters are bursting with flowers and herbs all summer. (We had a snow flurry on June 1st this year so summer started in July.) Fresh herbs are a must for my gourmet cooking. However, this season my parsley will come from the market because a hungry gray squirrel mistakenly thought it had been planted for him. This morning only a few stems remained. (The trap, where has that man of mine put the trap?) A tiered, cedar planter that David made for me is a stunning show piece with pink and lavender ivy geraniums, red begonias, creeping Charlie, hot pink petunias and white cascading bacopa.

If there is an open spot of ground (or not), a nasturtium seed has been poked in it. These hardy annuals attract the birds and butterflies, garnish my salads and bloom until the snow flies. Today is July 6, 2009 and the first blooms have opened, one yellow and one orange. Our first flakes of snow are usually seen around Halloween, so I get to appreciate the gay, bright colors of these pretty flowers for awhile.

Tonight there is just the slightest breeze and the heart shaped leaves of the quaking aspen are fluttering ever so gently. My Mountain Man should be home soon, so I spritzed on a little perfume, applied some lipstick, spit on my hands and patted down the run-away wisps of hair. Just kidding about the spit. I used hair spray. After a long day, I'm trying not to look like the last defender of the Alamo.

With mosquito repellent in one hand, a glass of wine in the other, and a pen and notepad tucked under my arm I head out to the park bench on the front porch. Staring straight ahead the scene is idyllic. In the foreground are young vine maples with delicate green leaves and red branches, Oregon grape with scalloped edged, dark green leaves and mugo pines that are reaching for the sky. As my eyes focus beyond I see the four-foot-tall spires of fireweed that are brandishing hot fuchsia colored flowers, the new growth of light green leaves on burning bushes and barberry with shades of pink to maroon leaves on long, gracefully sweeping branches. The chocolate mint and lemon balm that flourish by the step, add contrast with yellow and green leaves and chocolate brown stems. It smells so good. It is a playground for the sweet, little hummers. We do enjoy this time of year. Beautiful and quiet—this also is Mary's Place.

Oh, and it is Mattie's place too. She is currently curled up on a wrinkled rug at my feet. It takes a long time to get just the right wrinkle you know. Tonight it required about 15 turnarounds (seven to the left and eight to the right). The next step is to scratch and paw at the rug to build up the wrinkles for just the perfect napping spot. Her favorite green tennis ball of the moment, with the hide hanging half off, is nestled between her paws. Her graying muzzle gently rests on top of the beloved ball. She is still wet from her last swim in the river. What a happy dog!

It is now 7:25 p.m. Still no sign of David. Obviously he had to work late. The temperature is dropping and my arms have lots of chilly bumps which only give the mosquitoes a better target. I did apply repellant but they buzz and settle in as if to say "You missed a spot! I'm cold but I don't want to go inside yet. A Stellar Jay in his amazing coat of neon blue feathers has come to visit. A night like this makes all the effort of mountain life worth while.

The smell of a roasting chicken wafts from the open kitchen window. It smells wonderful and I'm hungry. To hell with the diet. ....

ROAST CHICKEN WITH YAMS AND CARROTS

You can use boxed stuffing or make your own. I like to make my own using cubes of bread, chopped onion, chopped celery—the leaves too, just a sprinkle of dried chipotle, poultry seasoning, salt and pepper, lots of fresh parsley and chicken broth.

Serves 6

3 cups seasoned bread stuffing
1 roasting chicken (about 7 pounds)
Salt and black pepper
1 package of rotisserie seasoning with the roasting bag
2-3 carrots washed, peeled and sliced into rounds
1 large red garnet yam washed, peeled and cut into chunks
1 can chicken broth (unless you have some homemade stock, then use that).

About 3 hours before you begin roasting the chicken wash it and sprinkle the inside with salt and pepper. Place the chicken in the roasting bag and sprinkle the seasoning on top of it. Squish the bag around a bit to disperse the seasoning evenly over the chicken and refrigerate. Prepare the stuffing mixture.

When you are ready to cook the chicken, take it from the refrigerator and remove the plastic bag. Spray a roasting pan with a no-stick cooking spray, place the chicken in the roaster and fill the cavity with stuffing. Put any extra stuffing around the chicken. Place the sliced carrots and chunks of yams around the chicken. Drizzle some of the chicken broth over the dressing and vegetables.

Put the lid on the roaster and place in an oven that has been preheated to 350 degrees. Roast until the meat thermometer inserted in the thickest part of the thigh registers 180 degrees. It will take about 2 hours, maybe longer. I like my chicken just about falling off the bones. Check it once in a while and baste with remaining chicken broth if needed so that it doesn't get dried out.

This is finger licking good and easy!

CHICKEN WITH FRESH APRICOTS

This is a great springtime recipe. The rich flavors run from fruity to peppery and cooking time is only about one-half hour.

I like to serve this with a crisp, cold Riesling.

Serves 4

16 whole blanched almonds
2 teaspoons unsalted butter
4 ripe apricots, pitted and quartered
1 tablespoon olive oil
4 chicken breast halves, boneless and skinless
Salt and freshly ground black pepper
1 teaspoon finely grated fresh ginger
1 scallion white and green parts sliced separately
½ teaspoon finely grated lime zest
½ Habanero chili, seeded and thinly sliced
½ dry white wine
2 tablespoons pure maple syrup

Preheat oven to 350 degrees. Put the almonds in a pie plate and bake for 8 minutes or until fragrant and browned; let cool. Crack the almonds coarsely with the side of a large knife.

In a large skillet, melt the butter. Add the apricots, cut side down and cook over moderate heat until lightly browned, about 3 minutes. Turn the apricots and cook for one minute longer. Transfer to a plate.

Add the olive oil to the skillet and heat until shimmering. Season the chicken breasts with salt and pepper and add to the skillet. Cook over moderately high heat until browned, about 3 minutes. Turn the chicken and cook over moderately low heat until just white throughout, about 7 minutes longer. Transfer the chicken to the plate with the apricots.

Add the ginger, scallion whites, lime zest, and chili to the skillet and cook stirring for 30 seconds. Add the wine and simmer over moderately high heat, scraping up the browned bits from the bottom of the skillet. Add the maple syrup, apricots and chicken and simmer just until heated through; season with salt and pepper.

Transfer the chicken to plates and spoon the sauce on top. Sprinkle with the cracked almonds and scallion greens and serve.

COME TO MARY'S PLACE AND PLAY

It is August 2009. The pinecone harvest has begun and there are "pitchy" little squirrels running everywhere I look as I make my way down the lane to the gift shop. Each is proudly brandishing a freshly cut pinecone to take home and save for a cold winter night's dinner.

There is definitely a chill in the air and my sweater was needed for the morning walk to work. Every time I unlock the front door and enter my little shop full of fun and fancy, I stop for a moment and appreciate all that it stands for. The gift shop has evolved over a period of five years. I, myself, have evolved and grown to be a better person over the last 10 years of my life in the mountains.

My husband has actually been the instigator of pretty much all of my projects. He seems to think that I lack for things to do ... well not anymore!

One lazy spring Saturday afternoon as we are enjoying the hot tub and doing absolutely nothing, he says to me, "You need to write a cookbook. You're a great cook. I think that you should write a cookbook." So I did…

Another quiet and peaceful afternoon sitting by the river and soaking up the magnificent view, he says, "You know your jams and sauces are really good. I think you should market them." So I got FDA/USDA certified, obtained all necessary licenses and a food handler's permit. There were many appointments, meetings with various state and county officials, and inspection to go through. After all of the hoops were jumped through and all of the I's were dotted and T's were crossed, I now make and sell jams, preserves, jellies, seasoning blends, and salad dressings. I also have a line of bread, cookie, scone and muffin mixes. All have my North Woods brand on them. One idea seems to breed another. ...

One night, David inserted a movie into the DVD player and we snuggled into the couch with popcorn and wine (great combination) to escape reality for a couple of hours. Suddenly the movie stopped playing. Silly me, thinking that he had sat on one of the four remotes (none of which

I am allowed to touch) and inadvertently hit the stop button, I elbowed him and said, "Hey, turn the movie back on." He looked at me and said, "SOAP, I think you should make soap." So I purchased books, studied soap making and experimented with many mediums, colors, fragrances and styles. Now my North Woods brand is on soaps, lotions, bath salts, bubble bath, and lip balm.

People like to eat. Actually, it is my second favorite sport. A leisurely Sunday brunch prompted the promotion of product by samplings of my fresh, homemade bread with my fresh homemade jams. It was a good thought and customers love it. However, it did create a lot of extra work and lots of dishes at the end of the day.

Somehow these simple teas grew into 6-7 course formal high teas. The "Powder Room" is full of fun hats, feather boas, and a looking glass mirror. The ladies dress for "Tea," take pictures, laugh, and have fun. Mary's Place is indeed a place to play.

The "Sunroom" holds displays of soaps, gourmet pastas and greeting cards. The "Main Tea Room" has two large oak dining sets and can seat 18 The "Lavender Tea Room" has lavender walls, sparkling and sequined lavender netting draping the windows, gourmet chocolates, a Christmas tree and a tea table for six.

Upstairs is the "Teddy Bear Loft". A large array of teddy bears fill this area. They are there to play with, hug, and enjoy. The loft also is home to an on-going jigsaw puzzle table and five comfy beds.

In July of this year, my first men's group stayed there. It was the groomsmen's side of a bridal party. They had BBQ by the river, watched the stars come out until about 2 a.m. and then climbed the stairs to the loft and slept with the Teddy Bears. The next morning, the tea table chairs were draped with tuxedos and the floor was covered with cookie crumbs from the two dozen Snickerdoodles I had baked for them. The Mom in me just thought that a group of guys should have cookies. Evidently, so did they.

David's next idea was for gift baskets. He says to me, "You have a good eye for design. You should make gift baskets." Now, I have drawers full of rolls of paper, cellophane and ribbons. There are boxes of raffia, paper and straw packing materials.

I have discovered that frogs like to play in ribbon spools. Many is the time that I have selected a spool of ribbon and had a frog jump out of it. The first couple of times gave me quite a start. I don't know how they get in the house. This particular work table is by the back door. The frogs must lay in wait for the door to open so they can hop in and play. Sometimes they just sit on top of the ribbons. When I reach for and try to pick up ribbon, and grab a squishy, gooey frog instead ... oh, that is just not right!

All of this began in our garage-sized guest house. Soon I needed more space and moved to the pink cabin. It had been empty for many years. We had purchased it two years prior but had done nothing with it. It was full of moldy bedding, old bits of crockery, and stale, smelly old furniture. The clean-up took over two weeks.

Not knowing what I would find upon entering, I had donned long, yellow, rubber gloves that came up to my elbows. Each pocket had a can of insect spray. My left hand had a sack of mouse traps and my right held a baseball bat. I cranked up some country tunes on an old CD player and armed as I was entered the dark interior of my new shop. If anything had run across the floor or dropped from the ceiling, I know I would have wet my pants and left the same way I came in, swinging the bat and spraying clouds of insecticide.

The pink cabin actually worked out quite well for me. It became filled with treats and surprises for guests. Every Thursday afternoon I held an open-house tea party for the neighborhood. It was a simple affair, just cookies and tea at 2:00 in the afternoon. The tea tables were set about 1:00 and I could set my clock by watching people coming from three directions toward the cabin for an afternoon of tea and visiting.

After my parents moved to assisted living in town, the house we had bought for them became the current location of my gift shop and tea house. The pink cabin is now "THE NORTH WOODS SOAPHOUSE."

As I'm sure you can see, there is no longer time to use the hot tub, sit by the river, be lazy, or sleep in. That is why I mentioned earlier that it is important to make the needed time for those activities.

If that loving husband of mine has one more great project for me, this will indeed be Mary's place because David will be gone. Out the door he'll be with my boot in his . . . well, you get the picture.

THIS IS WHERE WE WANT TO BE

So you want to live in the mountains, go for it. The serenity you feel while sitting by the river side can't be duplicated. The contentment and feeling of bonding with the earth as you stroll through the forest is overwhelming. Your footsteps release the scents of crushed pine and fir needles, damp mosses on the forest floor release a sensual muskiness.

Stand still for just a minute in a quiet spot and watch and listen. That quiet spot is teaming with life in tiny cities of a different kind. Turn over a rock and behold all of the life forms it protects. Savor the beauty and fragrance of a wild flower, but do not pluck it from the soil. Simply appreciate it for what it is.

Put all of these things together, create an adventure and live a dream of your own.

We have chosen after life, cremation and requested that our ashes be carried by a forest breeze across the mountain ridge behind our home. We will forever remain full-time mountain residents and will become the new friendly ghosts of the cabin.

RECIPE INDEX

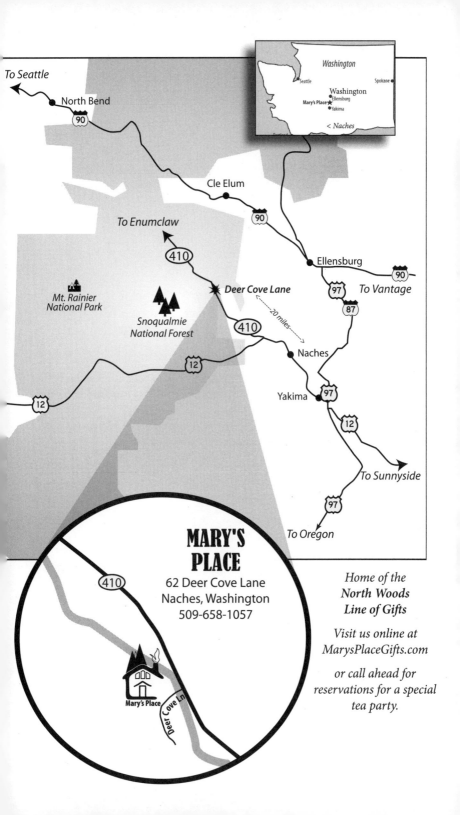

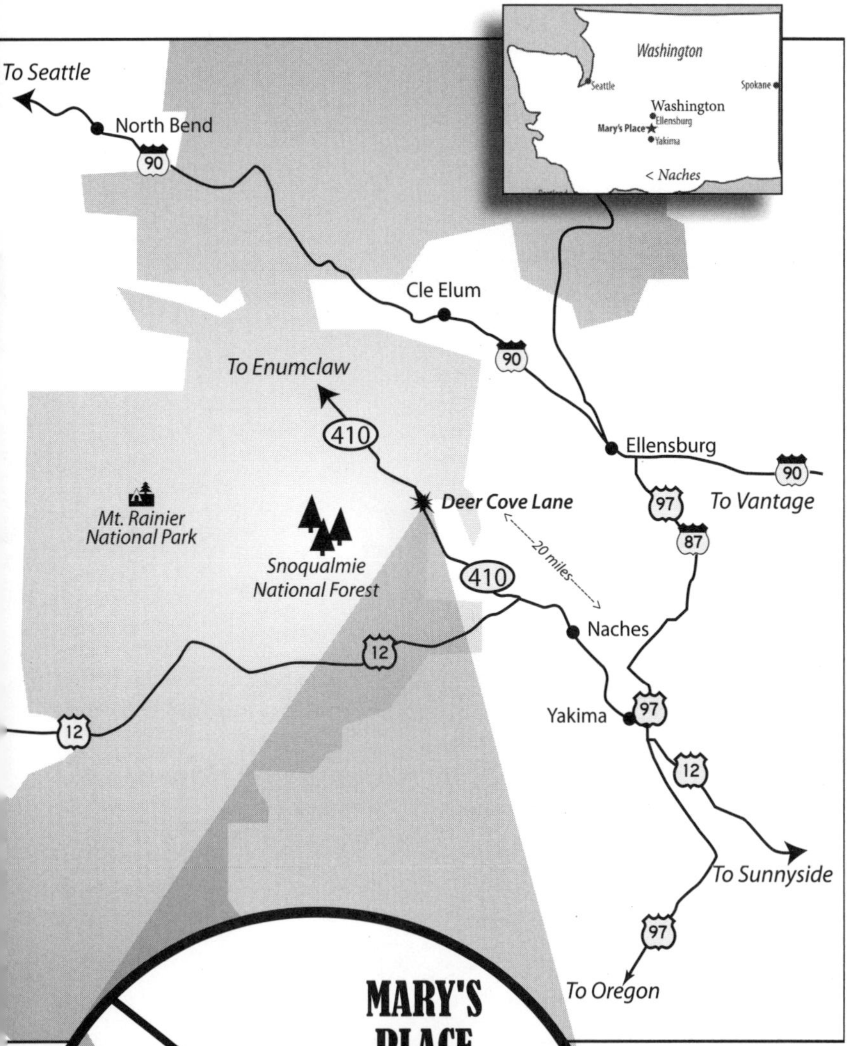

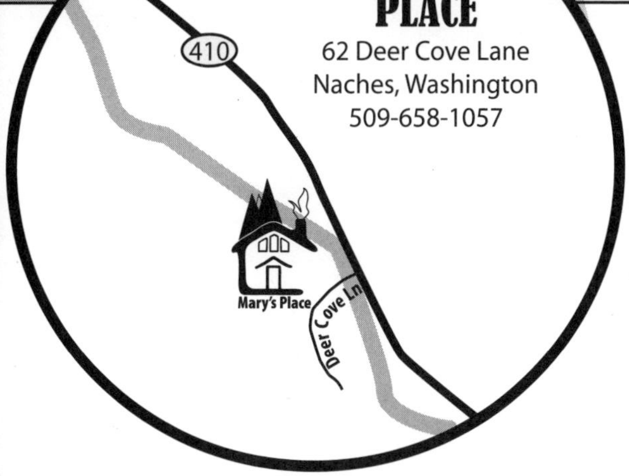

Home of the
North Woods
Line of Gifts

Visit us online at
MarysPlaceGifts.com

or call ahead for
reservations for a special
tea party.

Here's a tip from Mary:

Pop the book into a gallon-size zip-top bag, and voilà! The book stays open more easily, and the bag will keep it spatter-free while you cook.